A Tragic Deception
Life, Lies, and End Times

By

Vickie J Blair

NOTE
Unless otherwise noted, all Scripture references
are from the New Living Translation Bible.

Contact Address:
P.O. Box 6737
Banks, AL 36005
USA

www.vickiejblair.com

For

Jone and Bruce Gittinger

Dear friends for many years. We met on the mission field. They are faithful co-workers in the Lord.

Thank you to Chris Reeves.

She scrupulously edited this manuscript. She corrects and offers valuable suggestions for improvement.
She thought of the subtitle for this book.

As always, final editing choices are my own. Therefore, it you catch a mistake, that's mine, too.

Table of Contents

Part Three - End Times

Author's Note

My aim in writing this book is twofold: First, to demonstrate to the reader how the enemy, Satan and his demons, use deception to take us away from the purpose that The Lord has for us in this life. It gives insight into the world of schemes and lies which are used to deny us of our best life in Christ.

Second, to give the reader a clear and simple understanding of events, as described in God's Word, that take place from the time of The Rapture through to the City of God. It is my desire to present a clear timeline. It is not my intention to present various interpretations on what countries will make up the world alliance. While I make mention of those countries listed in Ezekiel 38 and Daniel 11, such as Gog being Russia, I do not jump into the debate on what countries are represented in Nebuchadnezzar's dream that is recorded in Daniel 2. Those ruling nations and time periods of rule are cause for much speculation. I say again, my aim is to give the reader an overall, easy to understand picture of End Times with encouragement to be ready, so as not to be ashamed when the trumpet sounds The Rapture.

Summary

Part One seeks to prepare the Christian to live victoriously and joyfully on earth before The Rapture, being aware of Satan's tactics, thereby, walking in the Light.

Part Two looks at the first three chapters of Revelation as Jesus warns the church, instructing them to be ready for The Rapture, unashamed at His coming.

Part Three addresses life for the Christian from the moment of The Rapture, and also, life for those left behind. It's an account of what happens during The Rapture, The Judgement Seat of Christ, The Tribulation, The Millennial Reign, The Great White Throne Judgement, The New Heaven and New Earth, and The City of God.

PART ONE

Beware The Enemy

Babes In Christ

Do you remember when you came to know Jesus Christ? You understood the reality of John 3:16, believed that God loved you so much that He gave His Son to pay the price for your sin, and you accepted Him into your life.

The act of believing and receiving Jesus Christ brought the Holy Spirit into your life. Therefore, you are sealed for eternity. Your salvation is secure. By receiving the Holy Spirit, you have thwarted Satan's goal to keep you from becoming a child of God.

Having failed in that attempt, Satan moves on to his second goal: preventing you from being effective in the Kingdom of God. He doesn't want you to grow into a mature Christian.

He wants you to remain a baby. Satan doesn't want you to be a light that attracts others to Jesus. He doesn't want you to be an example of living in joy and peace no matter the troubles of this world. Therefore, he launches an attack that will last all the days of your life.

It sounds miserable and daunting, but do not fear. God has given us insight into Satan's tactics as well as tools to fight the battles. Being good soldiers of Jesus Christ and maintaining a well fought battle will bring glory to Jesus and great joy to you.

Let's get ready for battle! Victory is promised to all who follow God's instructions.

How The Enemy Works

The beginning of any story is always a good place to start. Therefore, let's take a peek into the Old Testament book of Ezekiel to get the background of our enemy. In chapter 28 there is reference to King Tyre. He was an evil king also mentioned in the books of Isaiah, Jeremiah, Joel, and Amos.

Early in my Christianity I didn't fully understand something of vast importance in this chapter. I mistakenly thought the entire chapter was speaking about King Tyre, but I came to discover that beginning with verse 14, the narrative takes on a new thought. It begins to discuss a former Archangel named Lucifer, whom we know as Satan.

It seems Ezekiel is making a comparison between the evil King Tyre and Lucifer. Let's look at verses 14 - 19: "I ordained and anointed you as the mighty-angelic guardian. You had access to the holy mountain of God and walked among the stones of fire. You were blameless in all you did from the day you were created until the day evil was found in you. Your rich commerce led you to violence, and you sinned. So I banished you in disgrace from the mountain of God. I expelled you, O mighty guardian, from your place among the stones of fire. Your heart was filled with pride because of all your beauty. Your wisdom was corrupted by your love of splendor. So I threw you to the ground and exposed you to the curious gaze of kings. You defiled your sanctuaries with your many sins and your dishonest trade. So I brought fire out from within you, and it consumed you. I reduced you to ashes on the ground in the sight of all who were watching. All who knew you are appalled at your fate. You have come to a terrible end, and you will exist no more."

Astonishingly, we see that Lucifer, enthralled with his own beauty, attempted a coup on God. He actually believed he could overthrow God's throne. Added to this incredible attempt, he convinced a host of angels to follow him. Today we call Lucifer and the angels that pledged their allegiance to him Satan and demons.

It's interesting to note that it was pride that fanned the flame of the coup attempt on the throne of God. You're probably familiar with Proverbs 16:18: *"Pride goes before destruction, and haughtiness before a fall."*

Knowing the background of Satan's fall and that it was due to his pride filled heart, I can't help but question: are all sins rooted in pride? Is it pride when we disobey any direction of God? Are we believing our way is better? I leave you to ponder that with me.

There is something else we know about Satan. Jesus told us categorically in John 8:44b, *"He has always hated the truth, because there is no truth in him. When he lies, it is consistent with his character; for he is a liar and the father of lies."*

We initially see Satan in action in the book of Genesis. But first, let's look at what God did concerning mankind. In Genesis 1:26 and again in Genesis 2:15, we see God giving dominion to man over the things of the earth. He told them to reign over it, tend it, watch over it. Can you imagine how this infuriated Satan?

Satan had desired to rule over all. Therefore, he attempted to overthrow God. Having failed in his attempt, God threw him out of heaven and to the earth. God now makes things called human beings and puts these humans in charge of the earth! Satan must have been shocked and fuming. Why, he should be in control, not some mere human! Could it have been the result of his fury that caused him to tempt mankind to sin against God? We read of the sad event in chapter 3:1-13. Satan subtly begins in the first verse, asking the question, *"Did God really say you must not eat the fruit of any of the trees in the garden?"* His use of *"really say"* causes immediate question.

When Satan speaks to us like this we naturally begin to doubt. Did we hear correctly? Did we understand properly? Getting us to doubt ourselves helps prepare the mental ground on which Satan can launch attack. In fact, Eve becomes so rattled here that she misquotes God. She tells Satan that of course they can eat from all the trees in the garden, except the tree of the knowledge of good and evil. She adds that if they eat from that tree, or even touch it, they will surely die. The fact is, God never said they couldn't touch it, but Eve has begun conversation with the epitome of evil and confusion has entered her mind.

Next, Satan emphatically exclaims that should she eat the fruit, she absolutely will not die. It's just that if she eats from the tree, God knows she will then be like Him, filled with wisdom, knowing good and evil. So, what did Eve do? She considered what Satan said and made the choice to disobey God. She considered the lie, she believed the lie, she chose the way of the lie. Genesis 3:6 is revealing: *"The woman was convinced. She saw that the tree was beautiful and its fruit looked delicious, and she wanted the wisdom it would give her. So she took some of the fruit and ate it."*

There are three things Eve considered:

1. The tree was beautiful.
2. The fruit looked delicious.
3. It would give wisdom.

How, with his lies, does Satan tempt and deceive us? He knocks on certain doors that, sadly, we find easy to answer and open. Where do the doors lead? They lead to our mind. It is in our mind that demonic activity takes place, but these activities only come through a door that we open to them. The doors also include our physical senses of touch, taste, smell, sight, and hearing.

John warned us of this detrimental lie of Satan when he wrote in I John 2:15-16, *"Love not the world, neither the things that are in the world. If any man love the world, the love of the Father is not in him. For all that is in the world, the lust of the flesh, and the lust of the eyes, and the pride of life, is not of the Father, but is of the world"* (King James Version).

I also like verse 16 in the New Living Translation. *"For the world offers only a craving for physical pleasure, a craving for everything we see, and pride in our achievements and possessions. These are not from the Father, but are from this world."*

Look again at what happened to Eve.

1. She **listened** to the lies.
2. She **saw** the tree was beautiful.
3. She **touched** the fruit.
4. She **tasted** the fruit.
5. She believed it would give her great wisdom. One could say she **smelled** the fragrance of knowledge.

Satan never varies his tactics. He has been lying from the beginning. He will always lie, not some of the time, but all of the time. What can we do to prepare ourselves for such an attack?

First, let's take a better look at the doors.

We know that God is triune. He is God the Father, God the Son, and God the Holy Spirit. Three separate entities, but all one. You and I are created in the image of God. We are also triune. We are body, soul, and spirit. It is in our spirit where we invite Jesus to come into our lives. He comes by way of the Holy Spirit. Remember what Jesus told his disciples in John 14:16-18, *"I will ask the Father and he will give you another Advocate, who will never leave you. He is the Holy Spirit, who leads into all truth. The world cannot receive Him because it isn't looking for Him and doesn't recognize Him. But you know Him, because He lives with you now and later will be in you. I will not abandon you as orphans — I will come to you."*

The Holy Spirit comes in by our invitation. Revelation 3:20 illustrates this beautifully. *"Look! I stand at the door and knock. If you hear my voice and open the door, I will come in, and we will share a meal together as friends."* This denotes an intimacy with Jesus. We answer the door and respond by asking forgiveness of our sins with a desire to turn away from them. At that very moment the Spirit of God takes up eternal residence in our spirit and *"seals us unto the day of redemption"* (Ephesians 4:30 KJV). Our spirit cannot be touched by demonic forces.

The soul is that part of us that is the mind. It is where we think and make decisions. Demonic attacks come to our soul. This is where we open the door when the enemy temps, causes doubts, and lies to us. This is where the enemy can enter and take up residence, thereby influencing our walk with God, causing us to be ineffective. **I add here an important note: demons cannot possess a Christian, but they can reside in our soul (our mind, will, and emotions) and cause havoc to our spiritual decision making ability.**

Let's understand this further by looking at strongholds. II Corinthians 10:3-5 states, *"We are human but we don't wage war as humans do. **We use God's mighty weapons, not worldly weapons, to knock down the strongholds of human reasoning and to destroy false arguments** (emphasis added). We destroy every proud obstacle that keeps people from knowing God. We capture their rebellious thoughts and teach them to obey Christ."* The Greek word for *stronghold* is OX'YROMA. It means a military, strong walled fortress.

Now we begin to get a picture of how demons attack the Christian. When we crack open the door, just enough to consider the doubt or the blatant lie, we give permission for the enemy to squeeze in further. If these thoughts go unchecked, or unconfessed, the demon can fully enter through the door and take up residence in our soul which is our mind. Remember, they tempt through the senses of touch, taste, smell, hearing and seeing. These doors open the way into the mind where we make decisions.

What happens when demonic forces have come in through the doors to our mind? Everything opposite godliness begins to take place. We are no longer being influenced by the light but by the dark. When that happens, peace is replaced by depressive thoughts. There can be self loathing. Joy fades into despondency and can grow into bitterness. Courage is replaced by fear. When demons attack, it's never a pretty outcome. By contrast, peace, joy, and hope reign when the Holy Spirit is in control.

Look at what Jesus said to his followers in John 10:10, *"The thief's purpose is to steal and kill and destroy. My purpose is to give them a rich and satisfying life."* We may rightly ask the question: what does the thief want to steal and kill and destroy? He wants to steal your peace, kill your joy, and destroy your hope. When peace dissolves, joy fades away, and hope goes out the window. That is the goal of the enemy for every child of God.

Let's look at another example in Genesis. It's the sad story of Cain. Cain and Abel were the first two sons of Adam and Eve. Abel was a shepherd while Cain tended crops. Let's begin reading in Genesis 4:3-5. *"When it was time for harvest, Cain presented some of his crops as a gift to the Lord. Abel also brought a gift — the best portions of the firstborn lambs from his flock. The Lord accepted Abel and his gift, but He did not accept Cain and his gift. This made Cain very angry and he looked dejected."*

There are several points in this narrative that we could discuss, especially concerning the symbolism of the blood sacrifice; however, for the sake of our study, we will focus on the vast importance of the attitudes of the heart. Keep in mind here the doors through which the enemy may enter. When the Lord finds something unacceptable in our lives, don't we want to come humbly before Him and ask the Holy Spirit to reveal to us what needs to be made right?   That attitude is one that demonic forces cannot penetrate. A desire to be holy is a desire that keeps our doors closed tight.

This was a door that Cain didn't keep closed. God Himself approaches Cain and warns about the door. Look at verses 6 and 7. *"'Why are you so angry?' the Lord asked Cain. 'Why do you look so dejected?' You will be accepted if you do what is right.* ***But if you refuse to do what is right, then watch out! Sin is crouching at the*** door, *eager to control you* *(emphasis added). But you must subdue it and be its master."*

In the very beginning of the story of mankind, we see Satan's tactics. We see God's warning about those tactics, and we see what to do about it. God clearly and simply tells Cain that if he chooses to do what is right all will be well in his personal relationship with God. What is it that he must do to make things right? Ask forgiveness and repent. God's formula for peaceful, joyful, and hopeful living has never changed. Remember, the Scriptures tell us in Hebrews 13:8 that He is *"the same yesterday, today, and forever."*

What was Cain's sin? He did not give his best to God. Then, when God approached him about it, he refused to acknowledge his sin, thereby, refusing to repent. That attitude of heart opened the door for demonic activity to come in and work further.

The result of the enemy's work is evidenced in verse 8: *"One day, Cain suggested to his brother, 'Let's go out into the fields.' And while they were in the field, Cain attacked his brother, Abel, and killed him."* Cain had opened the door, demonic forces worked their evil, and murder resulted.

As we review this story, make note that Cain didn't wake up one day and think to himself that he would go murder his brother. No, it was a progression. Look at the steps:

1. He holds back his best from God.
2 He refuses to confess his sin.
3. Anger reigns in his heart.
4. Demonic forces enter through the

door of anger and unconfessed sin. Bitterness and jealousy are present.

5. Demonic forces whisper commands of murder.

6. Cain listens, considers, and obeys the darkness.

All of the above could have been avoided. As soon as Cain was admonished by God, he could have asked for forgiveness. As soon as he realized he was jealous of his brother, he could have asked for forgiveness. As soon as hatred began to build in his heart, he could have asked for forgiveness. This story is not one of sibling rivalry that turned into murder. It's a story of the results of unconfessed sin.

God is rich in mercy, always ready to forgive when we ask. Even after the murder was committed, if Cain had sought forgiveness, he would have received it. But he did not. In fact, his haughty attitude continued. Let's read the next verses, 9-14. *"Afterward the Lord asked Cain, 'Where is your brother? Where is Abel?" 'I don't know,' replied Cain. 'Am I my brother's guardian? But the Lord said, 'What have you done? Listen! Your brother's blood cries out to me from the ground. Now you are cursed and banished from the ground, which has swallowed your brother's blood. No longer will the ground yield good crops for you, no matter how hard you work! From now on you will be a homeless wanderer on the earth.' Cain replied to the Lord, 'My punishment is too great to bear! You have banished me from the land and from Your presence; you have made me a homeless wanderer. Anyone who finds me will kill me!"*

What a sad story. Rather than taking opportunity to confess and repent, Cain continues in sin, allowing demonic activity to work. Cain lied to God when he claimed that he didn't know where Abel could be found. Then, when God pronounces punishment, Cain is still in no frame of mind to confess and repent. His heart is so filled with sin that instead of showing any remorse for killing his brother, he is suddenly fearful that someone may kill him! What a selfish attitude - the result of unconfessed sin.

God in His mercy assures Cain that he will not be killed. God puts a mark on Cain (we are not told what the mark is) that will keep others from causing Cain any harm.

Then comes the most tragic verse of this story, verse 16, *"So Cain left the Lord's presence."* Sadly, there is no Scriptural evidence that Cain ever made his life right with God.

I cannot emphasize enough the importance of I John 1:9: *"If we confess our sin, He is faithful and just, to forgive us our sin, and to cleanse us from all unrighteousness"* (King James Version). Confession and repentance is essential to walking in Holy Spirit power. Cain refused to repent and gain forgiveness; therefore, he was void of peace of heart and mind. Instead, he remained angry at God for the punishment received. He didn't like the results of his own sin and blamed God for those results.

It is always interesting to me to listen to people's comments about God when bad things happen as a result of their own choices. I have heard people who claim to have no belief in God say that God must be a tyrant to allow calamities, disease, and disasters, especially as it affects them personally. Like Cain, they refuse to consider that the evil in their life is often of their own doing. They refuse to consider that God has actually sent a lifeline, through Jesus Christ, to anyone who will grab hold.

It's really so simple: when one is drowning, they can grab hold of the rope and live, or ignore the rope and drown. As that one is drowning, would it not be ludicrous to blame the person on the shore who threw the rope?

Cain refused to do what was right to save himself. Every person who has ever lived, and every person living today, has the same decision to make as Cain. We can choose to grab hold of the rope — or not. Cain saw the results of his choice. We, too, must see, and choose wisely.

There is another passage to consider what it reveals to us. Let's read the words of Jesus recorded in Matthew 12:43-45: *"When an evil spirit leaves a person, it goes into the desert, seeking rest but finding none. Then it says, 'I will return to the person I came from.' So it returns and finds its former home empty, swept, and in order. Then the spirit finds seven other spirits more evil than itself, and they all enter the person and live there. And so that person is worse off than before. That will be the experience of this evil generation."*

For a long time in my walk with God, this was one of those passages that I would read and have no understanding, so would just move on in the chapter. This happens with us all because we are all continually learning. It's with maturity and ever learning that we deepen our insight. I liken it to deep sea diving. When we are seriously searching out truth, we must arm ourselves with proper tools so that we may dive deep into God's Word and bring its treasures to the surface of our understanding. What are the tools? A good Hebrew and Greek dictionary. The Old Testament was originally written in Hebrew while the New Testament was originally written in Greek. Always go to the Hebrew/Greek meaning of a word.

Then, have on hand a book of Bible culture and customs along with a map of Bible geography. These tools help in bringing to the surface proper interpretation.

Now, back to the words of Jesus in Matthew 12. It always bothered me to read that the returning demon found the house (the person's mind) swept clean — and was so happy at this discovery that it invited seven more demons more powerful. This was one of my 'What in the world?' moments. Surely, I reasoned, the house is clean because confession of sin has taken place. That's why we have that wonderful instruction and promise in I John 1:9. We need cleansing!

Yes, but we don't need to leave the house empty! That's the whole point. When we confess our sins, receive forgiveness and cleansing, what is the imperative next step? We must fill our mind with the things of the Lord. We must fix our eyes on Jesus who is the author and finisher of our faith (Hebrews 12:2 KJV). A filled house with the things of God will keep the demons out!

What does fixing our eyes on Jesus entail? Meditating, praising, and praying. My favorite words on meditation are found in Psalm 1. When we read God's word, meditate on its meaning, talk to God, bring all our concerns to Him, and sing praises to Him we clean and fill our house. Then demons will come and find it occupied. A demon cannot stand true praise to God.

Examples Of Opening Doors

Opening a door to the enemy can be blatant, but more often, it's a result of demonic subtlety. The enemy is clever. His demons are equally sly. When they whisper their lies, they are convincing, even leading us to believe the lies are for our own good above God's plans of goodness for us. Reading that sentence sounds ludicrous, doesn't it? We quickly tell ourselves that we would never believe that Satan would have any good plan for us. Indeed, we would not if his intentions were clear, but this is part of his clever trickery; his subtlety is cunning. We are attacked and often don't even realize it. That is why we must constantly beware! Let's take a look at some true life examples (names have been changed.)

Pastor Bill

We've probably all been sad witnesses to such a story as this: Pastor Bill became a Christian in his early 20's. It wasn't long before he sensed God calling him into the ministry. He went to Bible College. He truly enjoyed the fellowship with other like-minded Christians. He delved into his studies and did well. While in college he met the most beautiful woman he had ever seen. Ruth was beautiful on the outside but equally so on the inside. Her walk with God was deep and sincere. She was funny, caring of others, and amazingly, according to Bill, she was just as attracted to him as he was to her.

They dated for two years. Upon their graduation he popped the question. At the end of the summer they were married. A year later they had the first of their three children.

His first church was a small gathering in the countryside. He loved the people and they loved him and his family. After a few years he was called to a larger church which thrived under his ministry just as the smaller church had done. God was definitely blessing his efforts. No one would argue that God had anointed him for such a ministry.

His wife, too, was loved and appreciated. She was a knowledgeable Bible teacher, holding studies for the youth one night a week, and also for the ladies one morning a week. God was blessing their joint ministry. Their children were happy and the oldest one had already made a profession of faith and had been baptized.

The evil spiritual powers of this world were not pleased. When Bill had been a young man, various demons had tried to tempt him away from becoming a follower of Jesus. They failed in their attempts. Therefore, plan B came into being.

Plan A is always to keep you and me from coming to accept Jesus as our Savior. If that fails, Plan B is to keep us from walking in the Light. Plan B seeks to steal our joy, kill our peace, and destroy all hope of being anything useful in the kingdom of God (John 10:10).

One Sunday morning after Pastor Bill had brought yet another helpful, encouraging, and challenging sermon, people were shaking his hand and thanking him for the morning's message. One woman shook his hand, held onto it while lowering her voice into a whisper and said pleadingly, "I need to talk to you Pastor. Is that possible?" "Of course," he replied, "call our church secretary and make the appointment."

This woman, we will call her Jane, also knew the Lord and had walked closely with Him for years. She, too, was married. She had two children. Her husband was also a Christian. He taught a boy's Sunday School class.

The evil rulers and authorities of the unseen world were having a meeting of darkness. The meeting may have been something like this:

> Relur, charge demon of the region, berated Senkrad who was assigned to implement Plan B in Pastor Bill's life.

"What's taking so long?" Relur hissed his disapproval.

Senkrad stepped away, out of reach of Relur's stinging tail that tapped in aggravated rhythm, ready to lash any victim of his choosing. "It took longer to set up Jane."

"What lies did you whisper?" Relur demanded.

"The usual," came a weak reply. "I suggested her husband had lost interest in her. 'Did he make much of your birthday?' I asked her, adding, 'He may not find you as attractive.' I further suggested to her that perhaps her husband only pays any attention at all out of duty rather than love. It seems she considered my words."

"What makes you certain?" hissed Relur.

"Because she went immediately to the mirror." He cackled in evil delight as he added, "I whispered, 'you know you're nothing compared to the other women in church. Look at the wrinkles around your eyes and your chin is sagging.'" Senkrad cackled again.

Relur displayed an evil sneer of approval. "Very good," he said as he rubbed his hands together. "Humans are easily caught in their own vanity. Continue on," he instructed Senkrad. "Lie about all her capabilities and put more doubts in her mind about her husband's love for her."

Senkrad saluted and slithered away.

Sitting in the pastor's office, Jane began to share that her marriage wasn't what it used to be. The pastor listened attentively, praying silently, asking for the Lord's guidance. While she was talking, Senkrad was whispering, "He used to kiss you goodbye in the mornings. Now he can't wait to just get out the door." Jane began to cry. Pastor Bill handed her a tissue. Jane took it, making certain her fingers brushed against his.

Nomed, a demon assigned to Pastor Bill, whispered, "Her touch felt nice, didn't it?" Pastor Bill continued his silent pleas to God, asking for guidance on how to best help Jane. He suggested that Jane and her husband attend the marriage course that the church held twice a year. "It's a course for everyone married, whether a marriage is in good shape or one in trouble." He took some leaflets and gave them to Jane. Standing, he assured Jane of his prayers for her and her husband. Sensing the session was over, Jane stood also. She was disappointed but promised the pastor she would think about the leaflet.

When she left, Pastor Bill sat at his desk and immediately prayed for Jane. He dismissed the suggestions from Nomed and called his wife just to ask how her day was going. He said he would see her at lunch. They each said "Love you" and hung up.

Nomed was livid, but he would not give up. Pastor Bill must be made to fall. He was too strong in his walk with God and too many people were making decisions to follow Christ. "Disgusting!" Nomed spat out the word as he followed Pastor Bill home to lunch.

As he entered the kitchen, Ruth was just pulling out a tray of buns. "I warmed them just the way you like them," she smiled and leaned forward for a quick kiss. He washed his hands at the sink and sat down to enjoy tuna salad on warm rolls with the woman he loved so very much.

Nomed whispered, "I bet Jane's kiss is soft and delicious." Pastor Bill blinked his eyes in astonishment. Where did that thought come from? He shook it away and continued his lunch, kissed Ruth goodbye, and returned to the church office.

Over the next several weeks, Jane saw Pastor Bill twice. She had not given the leaflet to her husband. She continued to wipe away tears in the pastor's office. He continued handing her tissues, once letting his hand linger on her touch. For the first time he considered her beauty and sweetness. He wondered about her husband's neglect of such a kind person as Jane, forgetting altogether that he had not heard her husband's side of things. Her husband, in fact, was unaware that things were not as they should be between them.

Relur, Senkrad, and Nomed hissed in evil delight! "Bill and Jane have both opened the doors and left them ajar!"

I'm sure I need not continue the story. You can guess the tragedy that ensued. It was just one door cracked open and left ajar. The enemy whispered lies. Both Bill and Jane listened — and considered! There came the mistake. After listening and considering, they should have implemented I John 1:9! This is a crucial defense. Without it, the offense wins every time. The enemy scores big time. Only I John 1:9 closes the door. Left open, the enemy strikes again and again and again until your joy, peace, and hope have been dashed to pieces.

Pastor Bill was found out. His marriage broke apart. Ruth was crushed, as were their children. Jane's marriage shattered into pieces. Her husband and children were also hurt and damaged emotionally. The church was crushed and it, too, was damaged. Many members left, disillusioned with both God and other Christians.

When we do something wrong and do not confess, "What I do doesn't matter. I'm not hurting anyone but myself" is one of the worst lies ever. Your unconfessed sin hurts everyone around you. Unconfessed sin with refusal to repent always matters!

Remember, the above story is true. Pastor Bill lost his family and ministry. He ended up working in a supermarket unloading delivery trucks and stocking shelves. Ex-wife Ruth went to work to try and help make ends meet. Two of the three children turned away from God. One of them got romantically involved with the wrong person. It all went terribly wrong.

The story of Jane is not much better. It took years before her children would even agree to see her. What precious years she lost watching them grow up. Her husband remarried a wonderful woman who loved Jesus. Together they raised Jane's children.

If only Jane and Pastor Bill had shut the door on the enemy.

Ramona and Greg

Ramona was 16. She went to a private Christian school and came to love Jesus very much. She was active in her church youth group and loved going to all the church services. Her parents and brother also loved Jesus.

One Sunday a new family came to church. They had a teenage son named Greg. The young people invited Greg to join their youth group. Ramona and Greg were quickly attracted to each other and began to date. He was also 16. They dated with other couples from church. They did fun things like bowling or hiking or having barbecues at each other's homes.

As time went by, Greg began looking for moments to be alone with

Ramona. It came when he invited her over for a meal with his family, but when she arrived she discovered that Greg's family were not at home. In fact, they would be out all evening. Greg explained that he just wanted to spend some alone time with the girl he loved so much.

He began kissing her and holding her too close for too long. Ramona felt uncomfortable. I Corinthians 6:19-20 sprang to her mind. *"Don't you realize that your body is the temple of the Holy Spirit, who lives in you and was given to you by God? You do not belong to yourself, for God bought you with a high price. So you must honor God with your body."*

She pushed Greg away, but he responded by assuring Ramona that they were honoring their temple. "We love each other right?"

"Yes," she agreed.

"Then, if we know we love each other, we know we'll be together forever, right?"

"Yes," she agreed again.

"Then, showing our love for each other is God honoring, isn't it?" (Demons who had been whispering these lies were cackling in evil delight.)

Ramona conceded. She was apprehensive, but Greg's words, influenced by demons, were convincing. She also heard the Holy Spirit whispering to take heed to God's Word. He reminded Ramona that God has a plan for good and not disaster.

Nevertheless, choosing "just this once" Romana succumbed to Satan's oldest trick, casting doubt on the Word of God. He used this trick on Eve. He used it on Ramona. He uses it on us all. Romana believed what Greg had said, that if they love each other then sleeping together is God honoring. What a terrible demonic lie. We must be aware at all times. We must *"hide God's Word in our heart that we might not sin against Him"* (Psalm 119:11). We must never forget that Satan *"disguises himself as an angel of light"* (II Corinthians 11:14).

We must remember what Jesus told us about Satan, that he, *"...has always hated the truth, because there is no truth in him. When he lies it is consistent with his character; for he is a liar and the father of lies" (John 8:44).*

Knowing the truth of God's Word, Ramona should have shouted a resounding "No!" She should have left that situation! She should have called out to God for help! She did none of those things.

Her relationship with Greg was never the same after that night. At the youth group, Ramona was laden with guilt. Greg grew angry and distant. They never spent time together again. In two years they both went to different colleges. Fortunately, they later got their lives right with God. They basked in His forgiveness. They knew that in God's perfect love and grace He has removed our sins (Psalm 103:12).

Yes, they knew God had chosen to never remember our sins (Hebrews 8:12). But they could not choose to do the same. For the rest of their lives, happy, used mightily of God, joyful in His forgiveness — they could never erase that memory themselves. It always remained a regret.   If only they had shut the door on the enemy.

Sheila

Sheila had graduated with a Bachelor's degree in Business. She then landed an intern position with a lucrative finance company that advised start up businesses and also handled stocks and bonds for their customers. She found her work exciting. There was always something new happening. She had never liked routine; therefore, the world of finance and start up businesses was right up her alley. She got along with all her colleagues. In fact, they all enjoyed each other so much that they often mingled outside of work. They had company picnics and softball games.

To pay for their social gatherings, they each put money in a box in the office kitchen. Employees could drop their donations in as they wished. Then, every month or two the money would be counted and plans made for the next company social event.

One day Sheila was in the office kitchen heating up her lunch. As she stood listening to the hum of the microwave her thoughts were drifting here and there. She thought about after work, stopping by the grocery store and the gas station. Suddenly, she remembered she had absentmindedly left her handbag at home. She had remembered on her drive to work, but it was too late to return home to get it.

Sheila eyed the money box. She could just take a twenty dollar bill out and replace it tomorrow. "Yes, go ahead just this once," a voice spoke into her thoughts. At first she felt a reservation. "It's not like you're a thief," the voice spoke again, "it's not your fault you got caught short. Go ahead." She agreed with the reasoning, took the twenty, and on the morrow forgot about it. Several days later, again alone in the kitchen, she remembered. Funny how no one had noticed any money missing, she thought, but why would they? It was an honor system and no one was required to put anything in. It was all voluntary to share in the company gatherings. Sheila couldn't understand it, but she began to feel compelled to take out another twenty. "There's so much in there," the voice of the enemy was easier to consider now. Why not? Who would know? It was rather exciting. She didn't need the money. She just enjoyed the thrill. She took out the twenty.

Unknown to Sheila, the person who handled the money checked the box every now and again. When enough was there it would be announced that it was time for another company fun time! The person keeping tabs on the money box began to notice that amounts were going down rather than up. A hidden camera was set up and Sheila was caught.

She lost her job. She lost her dignity. She lost the trust of her colleagues. She lost her own self respect; instead, self loathing set in. Sheila began a miserable downward spiral. She had no job references and began working at a convenience store. No longer able to afford her condo, she got a studio apartment.

A neighbor in the building often said hello to Sheila. They struck up a friendship and once in a while shared a cup of coffee and a chat together. The neighbor (we'll call her Mary) invited Sheila to visit her church. Sheila politely refused several times, but on the occasion of a musical concert at the church with refreshments afterwards, Sheila agreed to go.

The words to the songs touched Sheila deeply. The Holy Spirit began speaking into her soul, urging her to consider the truth of Jesus. "Jesus can change your life for the good," He whispered.

"No need to listen," the enemy spoke, "you're too far gone. You're useless." Sheila agreed with the enemy and tried to focus on something else, but the music and the words went deeper and deeper. Tears formed. She held her breath. How embarrassing. She didn't want to cry.

Just then, her friend Mary gently patted her hand and whispered. "It's okay. It's the Lord touching you." The Lord? Could it be? At the end of the concert a man stood and spoke about Jesus, why He had come, and that He was for everybody. He could take any life, forgive anything, and give hope and joy like no one else. Sheila was captivated. Other words were being pounded into her brain. "It's nonsense," the enemy spat out the lies. "No one can help you but you. It's all a myth."

Just then, Sheila heard the speaker invite anyone to come forward if they wanted to know more. Quickly she dabbed at an escaping tear. "I'll go with you," Mary whispered, smiling.

Sheila stood with Mary and together they moved forward where Sheila was met by another smiling woman. Mary stepped discretely aside. Sheila was captivated by what she was hearing. To the disgust of the mighty demonic powers at work, Sheila dismissed their lies and received the truth of Jesus. Sheila became a new person.

She stayed in church, learning properly how to counter-attack demonic lies. She also made right her wrongs, returning the stolen office money tenfold, explaining to her former colleagues how her life had changed. She never saw them again, but prayed that someone might consider her story and also consider Jesus. Sheila was learning, with joy and peace, to shut the door on the enemy.

iblical Examples of Opening Doors

We've already looked at Eve and her conversation with Satan and Cain's murder of Abel. Let us now peek at a few others to further deepen our understanding of how Satan works. His tactics do not change. That's a plus for us. It helps us know what to look for, how to be aware, and how to counter-attack.

Aaron and the Golden Calf

The story we look at now is recorded in the book of Exodus. As we begin our investigation, let's take note of something that happened in chapter 24, beginning with verse 9. It tells us something extraordinary. "Then Moses, Aaron and several elders of Israel climbed up the mountain. There they saw the God of Israel." In verse 11 we read, "Though these nobles of Israel gazed upon God, He did not destroy them. In fact, they ate a covenant meal, eating and drinking in His presence." How utterly amazing! Aaron and those with him actually saw God! I cannot imagine what that was like.

After their meal God told Moses to come higher up the mountain. Aaron and the others were to wait below. It was during this time that God would give Moses the Ten Commandments on two stone tablets and other instructions of which the people were to take heed.

Now, let's fast forward to chapter 32:1: *"When the people saw how long it was taking Moses to come back down the mountain, they gathered around Aaron. 'Come on,' they said, 'make us some gods who can lead us. We don't know what happened to this fellow Moses, who brought us here from the land of Egypt.'"*

What?! After witnessing God part the Red Sea for them to cross over on dry land and after eating and drinking by provision of God's miraculous hand, they get tired of waiting so they want to discard Him? This is another of what I call my personal "What in the world?!" moments.

Even so, as astonishing as this is to ponder, it is nothing compared to what happened next. In verse 2 we read, *"So Aaron said, 'Take the gold rings from the ears of your wives and sons and daughters, and bring them to me.'"* Verse 4: *"Then Aaron took the gold, melted it down, and molded it into the shape of a calf. When the people saw it, they exclaimed, 'O Israel, these are the gods who brought you safely out of the land of Egypt!"*

Do you find this mystifying? Aaron had seen God! Aaron ate with God! Aaron knew the truth of God because He had personally been with Him! How could he cave in like that just because the people were whining about having to wait?

At this point, let's stop and imagine what happened. Unlike the story of Eve and the serpent, we do not have a recorded conversation between Satan and Aaron. However, we know Satan's tactics. We know he appeals to our senses and to our own vanity. Therefore, we can make an educated guess as to the battle that took place in Aaron's mind.

The people were complaining. On and on it went. Constant nagging is hard for anybody. While the people were tired of waiting on Moses, do we believe that Aaron was, also? I find it hard to imagine, considering that Aaron had seen God and spent time with Him not so long ago. Aaron also knew that God instructed Moses to come up the mountain and told Aaron and the others to wait below. The people said they wanted another god, a god made with human hands, something tangible. Do we really believe that Aaron, after seeing God for himself, suddenly decides that what he saw wasn't real? Based on Aaron's experience, it seems extremely unlikely to have been the case. So, what makes sense?

Imagine this: as the people are nagging and Aaron is growing weary with their monotonous complaints, demonic powers see their moment to strike. They begin with false comfort. Perhaps they whispered something like, "You've been so faithful. The people are ungrateful. Why not give them what they want? They deserve what they get." Hmmmm, Aaron may have considered. Why should I encourage the people yet again? Time after time they are blessed and yet they grumble. "That's right," the demons whisper, "Just forget them. Mold a god for them. Leave them to it. Be done with them." In his frustration with the nagging people, Aaron listened, considered, and agreed to the demonic plan.

We know, later on when Moses directly questioned Aaron in Exodus 32, Aaron answered pitifully in verse 22, *"Don't get so upset, my lord. You yourself know how evil these people are. They said to me, 'Make us gods who will lead us.'"* Aaron is blaming his sin on the others. Don't we do that? We don't want it to be our fault. We like to blame someone else. Somehow it helps ease our feelings of guilt.

At this point, Aaron has opened the door even wider for demons to come into the living room of his mind. They quickly make themselves at home, wreaking more havoc. We know this because of something else Aaron told Moses about the incident.

Exodus 32:4 tells us, *"Then Aaron took the gold, melted it down, and molded it into the shape of a calf."* However, in his discourse with Moses concerning the gold given, he says in verse 24, *"When they brought it to me, I simply threw it into the fire — and out came this calf!"* If not so tragically pathetic, that would be hilarious. Think about what Aaron is actually attempting to get Moses to believe — he simply threw the gold in the fire and 'poof!' out came the calf. Not his fault? It just happened? Sound familiar? Haven't we all had times of not only putting the blame on someone else, but when that excuse appears not to be working, then, by some unknown influence — poof! — it just happened. Imagine that!

Demonic voices were whispering big time! They may have said something like, "Moses doesn't understand what pressures you have been under. He left you alone with this responsibility while he was off having a great time with God. You're not to blame. Just tell him what happened was out of your control." Once again, Aaron agreed with demonic influences and behaved accordingly. Aaron was digging a bigger hole with each lie he told.

What should he have done? He should have confessed right away! No doubt the verse I quote the most is I John 1:9, "*If we confess our sins, He is faithful and just to forgive us our sins and cleanse us from all unrighteousness"* (King James Version). There is nothing so horrible that God won't forgive when we truly repent. However, there would be no need to wallow in the degradation of sin, nor any need to go through the heartbreak of repentance, nor the need to endure the consequence of our sin, (especially when that sin has affected not only ourselves but those around us) if we had kept the door closed in the first place.

This incredible and heartbreaking story does not end here. *"Moses saw that Aaron had let the people get completely out of control, much to the amusement of their enemies"* (Exodus 32:25). While we may assume that the enemies are neighboring tribes that had been aware of what had been happening, we can also assume the enemies are those demonic forces at work. They would have been dancing in evil delight.

Suddenly, Moses stands at the entrance to the camp and shouts in verse 26, *"'All who are on the Lord's side, come here and join me.' And all the Levites gathered around him."* Let's take note here that the Levites, from the son of Jacob named Levi, were given the priestly position by God. The Levites were those who sacrificed the lambs on behalf of the sins of the people. The Levitical High Priest was the only one who, once a year on the Day of Atonement, entered the Holy of Holies to present a sacrifice on behalf of the Jewish nation.

When the Levites stood with Moses that day, they were commanded to kill everyone else in the camp.   About

3000 died that day. What a horrible consequence of sin. God sees holiness as extremely serious. There is no grey area with God. You are either for Him or against Him. Jesus said that very thing in Matthew 12:30, *"Anyone who isn't with me opposes me, and anyone who isn't working with me is actually working against me."*

I wonder how Aaron felt during this terrible consequence. I imagine he felt responsible. He probably had some "if only's" swirling in his mind. If only he had stood his ground and not given in to the people. If only he hadn't let their nagging weaken his resolve. If only he had continually spoken encouragement to them. If only. It would have been an entirely different story.

It would be easy at this point to become angry with Aaron. Why was he saved from this terrible consequence? He should have been the first to be killed. Here we see the unexplainable, undeserved, but beautiful grace of God. When given the opportunity, Aaron stood with Moses, being counted as on the Lord's side. Therefore, he was spared the punishment he deserved.

It is no different for you and me. We sin, often willfully. We deserve separation from God for eternity. We deserve death. However, we are given the opportunity to repent, to choose to stand on God's side. Therefore, by grace alone, we are saved. Paul tells us one of the most important truths of Christianity in Ephesians 2:8-9: *"God saved you by His grace when you believed. And you can't take credit for this; it is a gift from God. Salvation is not a reward for the good things we have done, so none of us can boast about it."*

By the way, let's not think for a moment that Aaron's action had no effect on him. Do you think he ever forgot how many died that day because of the consequence of his sin, his appalling lack of leadership, and his refusal to stand firm for the things of God?

David and Bathsheba

This is one of the most well known Bible stories among Christians and non Christians alike. We're familiar with David strolling onto his roof when he gazes across the way and sees a beautiful woman taking a bath. Overcome with temptation, he sends for her and commits adultery. However, the story did not begin there. He did not open the door to a demonic attack on the roof. He had already weakened his resolve, cracking open the door to the demon's lies long before he saw Bathsheba taking a bath.

Let's take a look into Scripture to discover what happened. It begins in II Samuel 11:1, *"In the spring of year, when kings normally go out to war, David sent Joab and the Israelite army to fight the Ammonites. They destroyed the Ammonite army and laid siege to the city of Rabbah. However, David stayed behind in Jerusalem."* Nothing is recorded in God's Word as a filler or mere chance. Everything is for a reason. Doing some spiritual deep sea diving and going deep into His Word to bring His treasures to the surface of our understanding is so exciting. Such study gives needed insight to help us properly understand in order to apply what we learn to our own lives. Such truths help us to keep our doors shut.

So, what is so revealing about this verse? The answer is in the very last sentence: *"David stayed behind in Jerusalem."* You see, when you study the customs of the time, you will discover that it was common practice for kings themselves to lead their men into battle. It's clearly stated in the above verse where we read, *"In the spring of the year, when kings normally go to war..."* David was celebrated for leading his men into victorious battle time and time again. What happened on this occasion? Was he tired? Was he on an ego trip, telling himself he was now too important to dirty his hands in battle? We have no record as to why he made this decision. We only know he should have been with his warriors. He was definitely in the wrong place when he strolled onto the roof. God's plan was for David to lead his men into battle; however, he stepped aside from God's plan. David had opened a door. To open our door to the enemy at any time is always a dangerous move. The decision that David made may have seemed harmless at the time. So, he stayed home just once. These are thoughts that are whispered to us by the enemy. "It won't matter just this once," has been a deceptive lie whispered throughout history. When heeded, it brings spiritual tragedy — not some of the time, but all of the time. The very moment we choose "just this once" to disobey God we have opened our door to hear and consider more lies. Heeding those lies always leads to disaster.

So we see that David's spiritual resolve has been weakened by his own disobedience. Now it's easier for demonic influences to plan other attacks. The opportunity came on the roof. Had David been spiritually strong, he would have innocently strolled onto the roof, innocently saw the woman taking a bath, and innocently removed himself from that scene.

However, that innocence was now tainted. Demons were lurking, peeking into the now open door to his mind. The very moment he saw the woman taking a bath the demons began whispering, perhaps something like, "What a beauty. Wouldn't it be lovely to be with her? You've worked so hard for such a long time; you deserve her. Why, you're the king! Call for her! Reward yourself for your labors. It won't matter just this once." Remember, Satan's tactics are always the same. His lies always appeal to the weakness of our own vanity. David heard and considered. Demons lie to us and we hear it. The hearing we can't help. It's the considering that opens the door. When we are considering anything, we are meditating upon the matter. God's Word instructs us to *meditate on His word day and night.* When we do that we are then "*like a tree planted by the water that brings forth fruit in due season*" (Psalm 1). The fruits alluded to are the fruits of the Spirit like love, joy, peace, and more, listed in Galatians 5:22-23. When we do not meditate on the light of the Word, we are open to the darkness of this world - that evil realm where demons hover, looking for prey.

David had now made two mistakes. He disobeyed God by not being with his warriors. Then he considered the demons as they enticed him with the woman taking a bath. The now weakened David obeys the demons! Yes! He sends for the woman named Bathsheba and begins a sexual relationship with her. David is now treading dangerous water. He has been found in a spiritual sea of sin, drifting perilously far from the shore of God's truth.

Some time passes by when one day David gets dreaded news. Bathsheba is pregnant. Now here is another moment that David, being obviously reminded of his sin, could have repented immediately. But he doesn't. He listens to demonic whispers again! Perhaps they say something like, "You have to cover this up. You're the king. No one can know what has happened. It could ruin your reputation." Isn't that often the way for us? When we are on the verge of being discovered in our sin, instead of coming clean for forgiveness and making right the wrong, we make futile attempts to hide it. Futile, because even if mankind does not discover our sin, God knows all along. Endeavoring to hide it from God is actually a dangerous thing to do. Remember, sin affects not only ourselves but also those around us.

In both his state of panic and his refusal to repent, David sends for Bathsheba's husband Uriah. David assumes Uriah will go to his wife and have sexual relations, but he does not. Uriah is a loyal and excellent soldier. We read in II Samuel 11 that when David asked Uriah why he didn't go home to his wife, Uriah replied that he could not rest as long as those in his unit were still fighting. David then invited him to dinner and got him drunk. Still, Uriah would not go home. Instead of being touched by Uriah's faithfulness, David panicked even more. In his refusal to respect the character of Uriah, and in his desperation to cover his sin, he orders Uriah back to his unit with a letter to be given to the commander. In II Samuel 11:15 we read these horrible words, *"The letter instructed Joab, 'Station Uriah on the front lines when fighting is fiercest. Then pull back so that he will be killed.'"*

After Uriah's death, and Bathsheba having completed the required time of mourning in keeping with their culture, David sent for her. She became one of his wives and gave birth to a son. *"But the Lord was displeased with what David had done"* (vs. 27). Reading that sends a shiver through me. I never want to displease the Lord. We all sin, you may rightfully be thinking. Therefore, don't we all displease the Lord everyday? That line of thinking is something else the enemy uses. Demons may whisper, "Don't feel badly about what you've done. After all, you can't be perfect.

It's unfair of God to be displeased that you have sinned. It's not your fault. Why, everyone sins." These lies only distance us from God. The further we go from the Light of His love and forgiveness, the deeper we go into the darkness of despair and degradation.

You see, while it's true that we all sin, it's a tragic demonic deception to believe there is nothing we can do about it, so why try? Paul instructs us very powerfully in Galatians 5:16-25:

"So I say, let the Holy Spirit guide your lives. Then you won't be doing what your sinful nature craves. The sinful nature wants to do evil, which is just the opposite of what the Spirit wants. And the Spirit gives us desires that are the opposite of what the sinful nature desires. These two forces are constantly fighting each other, so you

are not free to carry out your good
intentions. But when you are directed
by the Spirit, you are not under
obligation to the law of Moses. When
you follow the desires of your sinful
nature, the results are very clear:
sexual immorality, impurity, lustful
pleasures, idolatry, sorcery, hostility,
quarreling, jealousy, outbursts of
anger, selfish ambition, dissension,
division, envy, drunkenness, wild
parties, and other sins like these. Let
me tell you again, as I have before,
that anyone living that sort of life will
not inherit the Kingdom of God. But
the Holy Spirit produces this kind of
fruit in our lives: love, joy, peace,
patience, kindness, goodness,
faithfulness, gentleness, and self
control. There is no law against these
things! Those who belong to Christ
Jesus have nailed the passions and
desires of their sinful nature to His

93

cross and crucified them there. Since we are living by the Spirit, let us follow the Spirit's leading in every area of our lives."

Therefore, we must never be deceived by the powers of darkness to believe there is nothing we can do about our sin. The Holy Spirit is within us to be our constant help along rocky paths. Whispers of the enemy may deceive us into thinking we got away with hiding our sin. It's true that others may never know, but one thing is certain, we can never hide anything from God. There is only one route to joy when we sin - confession and repentance. Choosing not to do so was David's initial mistake in his sin with Bathsheba and Uriah. Very importantly, if we do not make things right before God, we are in danger of losing our anointing to be used in His service.

Let's take a moment to look at anointing. What does it mean exactly, to lose our anointing? After all, there are stories of those in ministry who continued to preach and teach God's Word with people responding to their teaching before it was discovered they were living in some secret sin. How does that happen? Keep in mind, it's not a person's charm but the powerful words of God that bring people to repentance. We read in Isaiah 55:10-11, *"The rain and snow come down from the heavens and stay on the ground to water the earth. They cause the grain to grow, producing seed for the farmer and bread for the hungry. It is the same with my word. I send it out and it always produces fruit. It will accomplish all I want to, and it will prosper everywhere I send it."* God's Word touching and changing lives is not up to anyone's character or personality; it is only because of the power of God's living Word.

Therefore, it is possible to be in ministry for a time, speaking God's Word, with listeners being blessed. Even so, be certain sin will be found out. Tragically, the unrepentant person, though teaching God's Word, begins to go spiritually deaf. R.T. Kendall, in his book The Anointing speaks of such a person becoming stone-deaf.

There are sad stories in the Bible of those who had become stone-deaf, ignoring God's instructions for so long that they were unmoved by the very words they taught. They could speak God's Words to others but were stone-deaf in the ears of their own hearts. The words of God that at one time brought them to repentance no longer had that effect.

Be assured, at God's appointed time, when no repentance comes, that person will fall. Remember Saul who had been King of Israel before David? At one time he was used to prophesy in God's power, but pride caused him to think more highly of himself than he thought of God. Saul became spiritually stone-deaf. We know that because in I Samuel 28:15 we read, "'I am in great distress,' Saul said. '... God has departed from me. He no longer answers me...'" (New International Version). Saul could have repented, but he did not. Therefore, he became spiritually stone-deaf. He could not hear God. At this moment in Saul's life, demonic powers had won a great battle. They had taken up residence in his soul. Saul did not repent and clean the living room of his mind. Therefore, demons set up housekeeping and never left. Saul died a most miserable man.

It is imperative that we never forget — confession and repentance are essential to victorious and joyful living in the power of Jesus Christ. Without it the enemy wins, making us useless in God's service. There was an important difference between Saul's sin and David's sin. Saul refused to repent and was set aside from being useful in God's kingdom. David, by contrast, responded differently.

As we continue the story of David's adultery with Bathsheba and of his murder of Uriah, we see that God chose to bring it all to light. If David, of his own accord, would not come forward, then God would call him to account. The story continues in II Samual 12. God sends the prophet, Nathan, to expose David's sin. This is what God, through Nathan, says to David in verses 7-9: *"The Lord, the God of Israel says, 'I anointed you King of Israel and saved you from the power of Saul. I gave you your master's house and his wives and the kingdoms of Israel and Judah. And if that had not been enough, I would have given you much, much more. Why then, have you despised the word of the Lord and done this horrible deed? For you have murdered Uriah the Hittite with the sword of the Ammonites and stolen his wife."*

Verses 10-12 are ominous. *"From this time on, your family will live by the sword, because you have despised me by taking Uriah's wife to be your own. This is what the Lord says, 'Because of what you have done, I will cause your own household to rebel against you. I will give your wives to another man before your very eyes, and he will go to bed with them in public view. You did it secretly, but I will make this happen to you openly in the sight of all Israel."* Remember, our sin always matters and often affects those around us.

The consequences of David's sin do not end there. Read verses 13-14. *"Then David confessed to Nathan, 'I have sinned against the Lord.' Nathan replied, 'Yes, but the Lord has forgiven you, and you won't die for this sin. Nevertheless, because you have shown utter contempt for the word of the Lord by doing this, your child will die.'"*

Oh! Sin is a cruel master. Do not serve it! Its consequences are painful daggers in your heart. Ask the Holy Spirit, not once but everyday, to help you keep your eyes on the holiness of God and walk with a pure heart in all His ways. Confession must take place daily with a plea for the Holy Spirit to guide you, to remind you of a wrong path, to strengthen your resolve to live according to the Word of God. This prayer is a necessary tool to an intimate walk with God.

To David's credit, as soon as Nathan exposed his sin, he did not try to excuse or deny it. He accepted the Lord's punishment and he repented. How do we know that? Look at Psalm 51. David begins in verse 1 with,

"Have mercy on me, O God, because of your unfailing love. Because of your great compassion, blot out the stain of my sins." Then in verse 14 he says, *"Forgive me for shedding blood..."* It's important to note here that he named the sin. Sometimes we are so embarrassed by our sin that we don't even want to say it out loud before God. Humble yourself. Name your sin before Him and ask His forgiveness. He will gladly forgive you and wash you clean. He loves you.

To be sure, the whispers of the enemy can even come when we are on the verge of confession. The enemy may say something like, "No need to confess. God knows you feel bad. Just carry on and try to do better." The enemy knows that confession restores our fellowship with God. The enemy despises the very thought because with fellowship we begin to be strong again with the strength of the Lord. Always beware of the lies of the enemy. To abide by them leads to great despair and interminable tragedy.

Ananias and Sapphira

We have looked at several Old Testament examples of Satan's tactics. Let's now take a look at an incident in the New Testament. The story begins in Acts 5:1-2. "But there was a certain man named Ananias who, with his wife, Sapphira, sold some property. He brought part of the money to the apostles, claiming it was the full amount,   with his wife's consent. He kept the rest."

The next verse is the focus of our study. Peter asks in verse 3, *"Ananias, why have you let Satan fill your heart? You lied to the Holy Spirit, and you kept some of the money for yourself."* Peter goes on to say in verse 4, *"The property was yours to sell or not to sell, as you wished. And after selling it, the money was also yours to give away. How could you do a thing like this? You weren't lying to us, but to God!"*

Ananias and Sapphira were consumed in pride. They were not giving for the love of God but for the love of themselves. They wanted the onlookers to believe they were so generous that they had given everything. In fact, they had a deeper love for money. Their egos were huge. They had greater desire for others to think of them as wonderful, selfless givers, than they did in what God thought of them. One wonders if they truly believed there was a God who sent His Son Jesus. Only God knows their heart.

As Peter pointed out, their sin was not mere deception to those in the church, it was a blatant lie to the Holy Spirit.

Did they really believe they could hide the motives of their hearts from God, or did they truly know God in the first place?

What happened next is a formidable example of the consequences of deliberate, unrepentant sin. *"As soon as Ananias heard these words, he fell to the floor and died. Everyone who heard about it was terrified" (vs 5).* I would have been terrified, too. The story continues in verses 8-10 when Sapphira arrives later. *"Peter asked her, 'Was this the price you and your husband received for your land?' 'Yes,' she replied, 'that was the price.' And Peter said, 'How could the two of you even think of conspiring to test the Spirit of the Lord like this? The young men who buried your husband are just outside the door, and they will carry you out, too.' Instantly, she fell to the floor and died."*

Can you imagine the utter fear? I have to admit that I'm thankful we don't literally see this happening today. Churches would be littered with dead bodies. Why did it happen to Ananias and Sapphira? Most likely as an example to us of the seriousness that God places on sin. There are always consequences, and when repentance fails to take place there is always death. Today, people may not drop dead before our eyes, but there is still death. Demons always win the battle, stealing away our joy, peace, and hope when there is no confession and repentance.

Peter

Peter is used by God to pronounce judgement in the story of Ananias and Sapphira, but now let's take a look at something that had once taken place in his own life.

The incident takes place shortly before Jesus is crucified. In Matthew 16, Jesus is explaining to His disciples that the time had come for Him to go to Jerusalem. He plainly tells them in verse 21 that He would be killed, but on the third day he would be raised from the dead. We can understand that must have been shocking news. Keep in mind, also, that at this point the disciples had no understanding of what Jesus was about to do - take upon Himself the sins of the whole world. They believed He was going to overthrow the cruel Roman government, returning power to the Jews to run their own country. Complete understanding of Jesus' mission would only come after His resurrection from the dead.

Let's read the next two verses, 22-23: *"But Peter took Him aside and began to reprimand Him for saying such things. 'Heaven forbid, Lord,' he said. 'This will never happen to you.' Jesus turned to Peter and said, 'Get away from me Satan! You are a dangerous trap to me. You are seeing things merely from a human point of view, not from God's.'"*

Understandably, we may feel a bit sorry for Peter here. After all, it was true that he simply didn't understand. He meant well. He was trying to encourage Jesus. We may then, also reasonably, think that Jesus was rather harsh with His reproach. Not so. Jesus was not actually talking to Peter.

Whom did He address? Satan. When Jesus said, *"Get away from me Satan,"* He was literally speaking to Satan! At this moment in time, Satan Himself, always seeking to destroy Jesus, had found a crack in Peter's door. Satan would have been searching hard, eyes on the door to Peter's mind, ready to enter with a lying attack.

Remember what Jesus had said to Peter earlier in this same chapter, verse 18: *"Now I say to you that you are Peter (which means rock) and upon this rock I will build my church, and all the powers of hell will not conquer it."* Hearing Jesus' plans for Peter must have made Satan livid.

Therefore, Satan lurked, watching, waiting for Peter to open the door to his mind just a crack.

The moment came quickly. Remember, Satan's tactics are always the same. He always lies. When Jesus declared the truth that He would be killed and rise again on the third day, we can conclude that Satan immediately whispered to Peter, "That can't be true. He won't be killed. Why, you'll be His protector, Peter. Tell Him." Peter listened to the lie, considered the lie, and acted upon the lie. He refused God's Word as truth. Eve had done the same thing in the Garden of Eden. Oh, Satan is more awful than I can think of words to describe him. So we see, Jesus wasn't being cruel to Peter. He was addressing Satan.

There is a passage in Luke 22:31-34 that we must read. (Remember Peter was first named Simon.) Jesus says, *"'Simon, Simon, Satan has asked to sift each of you like wheat. But I have pleaded in prayer for you, Simon, that your faith should not fail. So when you have repented and turned to me again, strengthen your brothers.' Peter said, 'Lord, I am ready to go to prison for you, and even to die with you.' But Jesus said, 'Peter, let me tell you something. Before the rooster crows tomorrow morning, you will deny three times that you even know me.'"*

When we read this account and the verses that follow where, indeed, Peter denies ever knowing Jesus, we can feel great sorrow, perhaps even surprise in what Peter did. However, when we dive a little deeper we see the grace of God, the mercy of God, the encouragement of God.

Jesus was encouraging Peter and believed he would repent. Upon repenting, in His grace, Jesus would forgive Peter. In His mercy, He would choose Peter to lead others to walk in the ways of God. Jesus would not give up on Peter even as he denied Him. Never forget, there is no sin so horrible that Jesus won't forgive when we truly repent.

I love the encouragement, too, for us all in verse 32 when Jesus tells Peter that He has pleaded in prayer for him. What? Jesus prayed for Peter? Does that mean Jesus prays for us? Absolutely! We read in Hebrews 7:25 that "*He is able, once and forever, to save those who come to God through*

Him. He lives forever to intercede with God on their behalf."

Peter failed God greatly, but he repented greatly, too, and God had a plan for him. God used Peter to spread the Good News of eternal life through Jesus. Indeed, he was used as a pillar in building the early church.

You and I can always be used, too, as long as we never forget — confession and repentance of our sin is a must! Remember, too, although the powers of darkness will never stop pestering you and me, God's strength will always be available to us to "*...focus on this one thing, forgetting the past and looking forward to what lies ahead. I press on to reach the end of the race and receive the heavenly prize for which God, through Christ*

Jesus, is calling us" *(Philippians 3:13-14).*

Points To Remember

1. Satan and his demons will lie, not some of the time, but all of the time.

2. When we confess our sins and repent, we will be forgiven, not some of the time, but all of the time.

3. When we realize we have opened a door to darkness, we must not merely repent and clean the house of our minds, but we must fill it with prayers, praises, and God's Word.

These points are key in walking successfully in the power of the Holy Spirit. When we are practicing these, Satan will not be able to steal our joy, kill our peace, or destroy our hope of being useful in the kingdom of God.

PART TWO

Preparing For The Rapture

Jesus Warns The Church

We must look now into the first three chapters of Revelation. These chapters precede the revelation to John of what would happen immediately after The Rapture, during The Judgement Seat of Christ, The Tribulation, The Millennial Reign of Christ, The Great White Throne Judgment, The New Heavens and The New Earth, and The City of God.

There are many Christians today, and I am one of them, who believe that The Rapture is imminent. More on that comes in Part Three of this study. For now, we look into the instructions Jesus gave which help us today to be ready for this event.

John wrote to his readers in I John 2:28, *"And now, dear children, continue in Him, so that when He appears we may be confident and unashamed before Him at his coming."* Jesus had something to say about being ready in His letters to the seven churches, as recorded in the second and third chapters of Revelation.

As further background, did you know that the return of Christ is alluded to more than three hundred times in the New Testament? It is mentioned eight times more often than His first coming, when he was born of a virgin, died for our sins, and rose again conquering death. Jesus Himself referred to his return twenty-one times.

Jesus longs for us to be ready for His return and not be ashamed in any way. What could cause us shame? Living in sin, having strayed from His

Word and from fellowship with other believers, neglecting God in prayer, thereby not hearing the voice of the Holy Spirit.

We will begin with reading chapter one as this sets the foundation for our understanding.You see, when the trumpet blows, sounding the time of The Rapture, it will be a welcome moment for God's children who are ready, but for those of His children who are not, that sound will bring deep regret. Please don't be one of those filled with regret. Determine to show your love for Him now, so that when Jesus comes for His bride, there will be only the greatest of joy. Paul speaks about this in Ephesians 5:25b-27: *"…Christ loved the church. He gave His life for her to make her holy and clean, washed by the cleansing of God's Word. He did this to present her to Himself as a glorious church without a spot or a wrinkle or any other blemish. Instead, she will be holy and without fault."*

The Revelation to John was given to him by Jesus Christ for the purpose of revealing the events that take place immediately following The Rapture. Those events are recorded in chapters 4 through 22. The first three chapters are to get us ready and to help us understand so we may share with others.

I've met many Christians who tell me they avoid Revelation because "it's too difficult to understand," and "it's too scary." Did you know that you are blessed just by reading the book? We are told this right away in Revelation 1:3: *"God blesses the one who reads the words of this prophecy to the* church, and He blesses all who listen to its message and obey what it says, for the time is near." Therefore, I encourage you to read, and to read with the attitude that the Holy Spirit will guide you into truth and comprehension.

We will begin with reading chapter one as this sets the foundation for our understanding. Revelation 1:4 greets us in this way: "Grace and peace to you from the One who is, who always was, and who is still to come; from the sevenfold Spirit before His throne." Two things to note from this verse. First, throughout the Bible the writers often open with "grace and peace." The Apostle Paul uses this greeting regularly. You will never see "peace and grace" written but always "grace and peace." Why? Because one cannot have the peace of God until the grace of God has first been extended. Therefore, grace experienced brings salvation, then the peace of God reigns within. Second, the sevenfold Spirit refers to the characteristics of God. (The number seven speaks of perfection or completion.) Jesus, of course, is holy and perfect; therefore, He has all of the Godly characteristics revealed in Isaiah 11:2: *"And the Spirit of the Lord will rest on Him — the Spirit of wisdom and understanding, the Spirit of counsel and might, the Spirit of knowledge and the fear of the Lord."*

Let's continue verse by verse through the first three chapters of Revelation to help us gain more understanding.

1:5b-6, *"All glory to Him who loves us and has freed us from our sins by shedding His blood for us. He has* *made us a Kingdom of priests for God His Father. All glory and power to Him forever and ever! Amen!"*

What a wonderful reminder of the undeserved, but freely given gift from Jesus to us, of eternal salvation. This book of Revelation is written to God's children who have experienced this amazing gift.

1:7, *"Look! He comes with the clouds of heaven. And everyone will see Him — even those who pierced Him. And all the nations of the world will mourn for Him. Yes! Amen!"*

This refers to the Second Coming of Jesus when He sets His feet on the Mount of Olives in Jerusalem. We know that because the verse tells us that every eye will see Him. At the time of The Rapture, only Christians will see Him, disappear from the earth, and join Him in the clouds.

What a sad comment that *"all the nations of the world will mourn for Him."* It will be at this moment that the enemies of Jesus, battling along with the Antichrist and the false prophet, will see Jesus in astonishing, breathtaking glory. An unimaginable fear will sweep through them as they realize Jesus is truly real, and they have lost the war waged against Him and His people.

1:8, *"'I am the Alpha and the Omega — the beginning and the end,' says the Lord. 'I am the One who is, who always was, and who is still to come — the Almighty One.'"*

This is, indeed, a declaration of the majesty and glory of Jesus.

1:9-11, "I, John, your brother and your partner in suffering and in God's Kingdom and in the patient endurance to which God calls us. I was exiled to the island of Patmos for preaching the Word of God and for my testimony about Jesus. It was the Lord's Day, and I was worshipping in the Spirit. Suddenly, I heard behind me a loud voice like a trumpet blast. It said, 'Write in a book everything you see, and send it to the seven churches in the cities of Ephesus, Smyrna, Pergamum, Thyatira, Sardis, Philadelphia, and Laodicea.'"

I find this passage so encouraging to my own walk with God when things are tough. Think about John and the situation in which he found himself. He was the leading elder for the Church throughout what is today the country of Turkey. He committed no crime, yet he had been arrested, charged, and given a sentence of exile. The Roman authorities stated his allegiance to Jesus as treason to Rome. Exile was considered by some to be worse than death. At least with death, the agony is over in a moment, but with exile the solitary confinement could last for years.

I've had the privilege of visiting the Island of Patmos, one of the Greek Islands. It is a small island of 13 square miles. Today only about 2000 people live there. They are all involved in tourism with cafes and bed and breakfast lodgings. There is a mountainous area in the center where a cave is located. It is believed that John spent his exile in this cave. While that can't be known for sure, it certainly is possible.

When John was exiled to Patmos, there were no other inhabitants, except for a garrison of soldiers to guard the island, making certain their prisoner would not escape nor would anyone come to his rescue. Imagine the loneliness with no friends whatsoever. His only human contact would have been with his guards and, we can assume, an occasional letter carried on Roman ships that brought supplies to the soldiers stationed there.

John was in a terrible predicament; yet, we do not read of any depression or any plans to escape. I have sometimes thought, if it were me, I might be trying to make a raft to float out to some passing ship in hopes of finding freedom. Not so with John. What do we read? As it was the Lord's Day, most likely meaning Sunday, the day of Jesus' resurrection, John was worshipping. He wasn't planning how to make a raft to drift away to freedom. He wasn't complaining to the Lord. He was worshipping his Lord. Even in this severe situation he chose to worship. As a result of his heart bent on worship, God chose to give John one of the greatest honors ever! Jesus would give John a glimpse into what was to come after The Rapture. John was instructed to write it down, which would become the book of Revelation that will last for eternity! Never would there be such an amazing bestseller that would stay on the top of the list for all time.

John was a man of great faith, great loyalty to Jesus, great trust in God's way; therefore, John was greatly honored by Jesus. John made a choice to worship God no matter what was taking place in his physical world. Worship and trust in God, for John, was not dependent on outward circumstances. He is an example to us today to keep our hearts in attitudes of worship no matter what turmoil exists in our personal worlds.

1:12-16, *"When I turned to see who was speaking to me, I saw seven gold lamp stands. And standing in the middle of the lamp stands was someone like the Son of Man. He was wearing a long robe with a gold sash across his chest. His head and His hair were like wool, as white as snow. And His eyes were like flames of fire. His feet were like polished bronze refined in a furnace, and His voice thundered like mighty ocean waves. He held seven stars in His right hand, and a sharp two-edged sword came from His* *mouth. And His face was like the sun in all its brilliance."*

To clarify, we find further down in verse 20 that the lamp stands are the seven churches to whom Jesus will dictate His letters through John. Then John writes that standing in the middle of these lamp stands was someone, *"like the Son of Man."* John wasn't quite certain who this was at first. We can understand his confusion because John was seeing Jesus like he had never seen Him before.

John had known Jesus for three years on earth. He and the other disciples and countless followers had been with Jesus nearly 24/7 until Jesus ascended in the clouds to be with His Father. Therefore, of course John knew what Jesus looked like; however, he had never seen Jesus quite like this in all

His glory. Jesus was wearing white with a gold sash, a picture of His majesty. He had white hair which, throughout the Bible, denotes wisdom as in Proverbs 16:31: *"Gray hair is a crown of glory; it is gained by living a godly life"*

His eyes were like flames of fire, indicating that Jesus sees all. *"For the Word of God is alive and powerful. It is sharper than the sharpest two-edged sword, cutting between soul and spirit, between joint and marrow. It exposes our innermost thoughts and desires. Nothing in all God's creation is hidden from God. **Everything is naked and exposed before His eyes** (emphasis added), and He is the one to whom we are accountable" (Hebrews 4:12-13).*

Let us never forget that we can hide nothing from God. He sees straight through to the thoughts and intentions of our hearts.

His feet were like polished bronze which represents judgment throughout God's Word. In the Old Testament we read, *"Using acacia wood, construct a square altar 7 1/2 feet long and 4 1/2 feet high. Make horns for each of its four corners so that the horns and altar are all one piece. Overlay the altar with bronze"* (Exodus 27:1-2). The sacrificial altar of bronze was a place of judgment for the sins of the people. When they brought their sacrifice, they were then judged clean. Praise God there is no longer any need for us to bring a sacrifice as Jesus was our sacrifice for all the sins of the world - the only perfect and lasting sacrifice. Therefore, Jesus's feet of bronze lets us know that Jesus is the Judge. He will judge our good works at the Judgment Seat of Christ. He will judge those who rejected Him at the Great White Throne Judgment. (More on that later.)

His voice thundered in power, and holding the seven stars, or the pastors, in His right hand, a sharp two edged sword came out of His mouth, signifying everything is measured against God's perfect Word. Remember when Jesus began His earthly ministry. After being baptized by His cousin John, He went into the desert where He was tempted by Satan for 40 days. How did Jesus answer Satan upon every temptation? *"No! The Scriptures say, 'People do not live by bread alone, but by every word that comes from the mouth of God'"* (Matthew 4:4).

1:17-18, "When I saw Him, I fell at His feet as if I were dead. But he laid his right hand on me and said, 'Don't be afraid! I am the First and the Last. I am the living one. I died, but look — I am alive forever and ever! And I hold the keys of death and the grave."

We can understand why John fell to the ground, motionless! What a magnificent sight he had been allowed to witness. No doubt, as he gazed on the glory of Jesus, he must have felt so undeserving that he fell before the Savior of the world. Jesus speaks words of comfort reminding John there is no need to be afraid. Why? Because of who He is - the First and Last, the One who lives forever, the one with all power who alone holds the keys to death and the grave. When you and I read these words, we, too, can be comforted, knowing that this eternal Jesus is the glorious One, full of perfect love, whom we will live with for eternity. We can also be overjoyed in knowing that the keys of death that Jesus holds will never have anything to do with us because we are His own!

1:19, *"Write down what you have seen — both the things that are now happening and the things that will happen."*

The things that are now happening refers to the letters that Jesus will dictate to the seven churches in chapters two and three. The things that will happen are covered in chapters 4-22.

1:20, *"This is the meaning of the mystery of the seven stars you saw in my right hand and the seven gold* *lamp stands. The seven stars are the angels of the seven churches, and the seven lamp stands are the seven churches."* There has been much theological speculation over the meaning of the *"angels of the seven churches."*

I can only share what I have discovered in my own search. As I used my tools, the Greek New Testament and Greek Dictionary, I found that the Greek word for angel is angelos. Angelos means messenger. Of course, we know that angels are often given the role of being a messenger from God to a person. Perhaps the best known angel with this role is Gabriel when he was sent by God to tell Mary that she was chosen to give birth to Jesus as is recorded in the first chapter of Luke. Even so, I didn't have that "peace that passes understanding" in accepting that the angels of the seven churches were literal angels. Therefore, I searched further.

Always remember the promise in Matthew 7:7: *"Keep on asking and you will receive what you ask for. Keep on seeking and you will find. Keep on knocking and the door will be opened to you."* It's exciting to delve into God's Word, spiritually deep sea diving, to bring treasures of truth to the surface of our understanding. It was during this persistent search that I came upon Matthew 11:10: *"John is the man to whom the Scriptures refer when they say, 'Look, I am sending my messenger ahead of you, and he will prepare your way before you.'"* The word "messenger" is the Greek word angelos.

So, we have discovered that angelos can refer to literal angels who are messengers or to humans who are messengers. Both declare God's Word. Due to this search it is my own belief that "angels" in Revelation 1:20 is referring to humans, most likely the pastors of the churches.

Let us now look into the first of the seven letters that Jesus dictates to John to be given to the seven pastors of the churches in Ephesus, Smyrna, Pergamum, Thyatira, Sardis, Philadelphia, and Laodicea.

Letter To The Church In Ephesus

Ephesus was a coastal town. Therefore, it was a major trade city with ships coming in and out of the harbor. There were businesses conducting imports and exports. Vendors would also have sold their wares to the sailors.

There was another great attraction in Ephesus that generated much business - the Temple to Diana. This temple was so elaborate that it was considered to be one of the seven wonders of the ancient world. The temple was first dedicated to Artemis by the Greeks, but when Rome took over, they renamed it the Temple to Diana. Both Artemis and Diana were goddesses of fertility. Serving in this temple were women, also called goddesses, who were in fact, prostitutes. You can imagine that with all the ships coming in and out the sailors were constant visitors to the temple.

When the Apostle Paul wrote to the church in Ephesus, he told them, as we read in his letter, "*...throw off your old sinful nature and your former way of life, which is corrupted by lust and deception. Instead, let the Spirit renew your thoughts and attitudes. Put on your new nature, created to be like God — truly righteous and holy" (Ephesians 4:22-24).* As people began to become Christians, the temple began to lose some of its regular customers. Vendors who sold fertility trinkets and images of the false goddess Diana also suffered a drop in trade.

Paul, and the church in Ephesus, was hated for this reason. Even so, he encouraged them in his letter to be strong in the Lord, putting on all the armor of God in order to walk in His ways. He reminded them that they used to be slaves to sin but now they are made free by Jesus. He told them in Ephesians 5:1, *"Imitate God, therefore, in everything you do because you are His dear children."*

This is the background to the challenges faced by the church in Ephesus. Desiring that they be ready for His return, Jesus dictated a letter to them. This letter is recorded in Revelation 2:1-7 as follows:

2:1, *"Write this letter to the angel of the church in Ephesus. This is the message from the One who holds the seven stars in His right hand, the One* *who walks among the seven gold lamp stands."*

Remember, the angel is most likely the pastor of the church. Jesus declares Himself to be the One who holds the seven stars, who are the seven pastors, in His right hand.

Did you know there are more than 100 verses in the Bible about the right hand? Culturally speaking, the right hand is significant. In that part of the world at that time, and in fact, in some parts of the world still today, the right hand is the clean hand. It is the hand used to eat. One would never touch food with the left hand because the left hand is used to take care of personal toilet needs. The left hand is the dirty hand.

There is a lovely verse in Isaiah 41:10 that reads, *"Don't be afraid, for I am with you. Don't be discouraged, for I am your God. I will strengthen you and help you. I will hold you up with my victorious right hand."* The mention of the right hand is also a reference to a clean and holy hand.

Jesus is encouraging the church's pastor here, and it's also an encouragement today. Pastors are held by God's own right hand. They are protected. They need not fear the difficulties and challenges that face them because God's own hand of protection and courage is holding them. It is the same with you and me. Whatever difficult path we may travel, God's own hand is holding us up. In God's hand we may lean into His strength to carry us through, to lead us onward.

2:2-3, *"I know all the things you do. I have seen your hard work and your patient endurance. I know you don't tolerate evil people. You have examined the claims of those who say they are apostles but are not. You have discovered they are liars. You have patiently suffered for me without quitting."*

Jesus begins by praising them for the right things they are doing. They are patiently enduring difficulties. They are not tolerating evil, very likely a reference to those who worship the false god Artemis or Diana. Also, they are aware of those making false claims of apostleship. Evidently there were some coming into the church declaring they were sent by Apostle John, or Apostle Peter, or Apostle Paul; but in fact, they were not. They came into the church with the goal of stirring up trouble, weakening the faith of the true believers in Jesus. Even so, the Christians in the church of Ephesus displayed great discernment. The Holy Spirit revealed the false prophets to them and they stood strong against them. They were praised by Jesus for pressing forward and not quitting. Wonderful! Then we come to verse four.

2:4-5, *"But I have this complaint against you. You don't love me or each other as you did at first! Look how far you have fallen! Turn back to me and do the works you did at first. If you don't repent, I will come and remove your lamp stand from its place among the churches."*

Do you find these words surprising? Jesus had such praise for them in the first two verses, but then tells them they have fallen far. They need to turn back and do what they did at first. What's all that about?

I have a friend who is a therapist who works particularly with couples whose marriages are in trouble. I've always been interested in psychology. It was a minor of mine when I was at university working on my Bachelor's degree. Therefore, when we are together, I often talk psychology with her, asking about some of the issues she deals with in marriage counseling. She shared with me that once in a while a couple comes in telling her that the spark has fizzled. They can't think of anything outwardly wrong. There's no adultery. They both help with the running of the house and caring for the children. They are a church going family. On the outside everything is good, but on the inside they admit something is missing.

My therapist friend told me at this point she asks the question, "What did you do when you first fell in love?" The husband thought for a minute and answered, "Well, I know she likes Italian food. Sometimes I would make a reservation at an Italian restaurant we both liked. I would get there first and have flowers on the table." The wife said, "I know he's an avid football fan. Sometimes I would make him things with his team colors." The therapist instructed them, "Go back and do the things you did at first."

When they met again with my friend, the husband shared that he discovered their favorite Italian restaurant was still there. He made a reservation and told his wife, "Let's not go together.

I'll meet you there after work." When she arrived, her husband was at the table with roses for his wife. She was carrying a small box and said to her husband, "This is for you." It was a new T-shirt with his football team colors. They went back to what they did at first, and the spark was rekindled.

It's the same in our spiritual world. Do you remember what it was like when you came to Jesus, asking for Him to forgive your sins, and inviting Him to come into your life? What did you do? Were you so excited that you told everyone around you? Did you invite friends and neighbors to church? Did you leave tracts in restaurants? Did you listen to praise music in your car and at home? Is that excitement still within you, or like the Christians at Ephesus, you are behaving properly, but the spark has gone? Jesus encourages us to, *"Go back and do the works you did at first."*

How do we do this? Jesus said to repent. Tell Jesus you are sorry for outwardly doing good works without inwardly loving Him with all your heart. Tell Him you are sorry you let the spark fizzle. Tell Him you want to burn bright again. He will forgive you, and with the help of the Holy Spirit, you will be renewed and filled afresh with anointing.

What happens if we fail to do these things? Jesus said He would, *"remove your lamp stand from its place among the churches."* This statement is not about salvation; it is about anointing. I cannot repeat often enough that once we are saved we are sealed for eternity.

However, if we do not repent and revive our waning hearts again, our zeal and spark is in danger of diminishing altogether. We are in danger of being ashamed at Jesus' coming, embarrassed that He finds us in a compromised position without the Holy Spirit's anointing. We don't want to be found in that predicament. Therefore, Jesus encourages us to examine our hearts and go back to that place when we first fell in love with Him.

2:6, *"But this is in your favor. You hate the deeds of the Nicolaitans just as I do."*

Here, Jesus compliments them again, praising them that they are aware of the deeds of the Nicolaitans and that they hate their deeds. Who were the Nicolaitans? They were a cult, seeking to infiltrate the church, distorting God's Word.

Many of you are old enough to remember the cult of David Koresh in Waco, Texas in the early '90s. Koresh knew God's Word very well but deliberately distorted it, and He did it for his own financial and sexual gain. His teachings and behavior were vile.

The believers at Ephesus were aware of such deception, hated it, and remained true to God's Word. They clung to the teaching of the true apostles and to the guidance of the Holy Spirit within them. This, too, is an example to us all. Measure all teaching by the Word of God. If it is contrary to His Word, stay away from it.

2:7, *"Anyone with ears to hear must listen to the Spirit and understand what He is saying to the churches. To everyone who is victorious I will give fruit from the tree of life in the paradise of God."*

This is a reminder that as we live in this physical world, hearing with our physical ears, as Christians we must always be careful to listen to the Spirit with our spiritual ears. An acute hearing comes by attention to God's Word with a meditative heart everyday, open to discern what the Spirit is speaking to us.

Jesus goes on in this verse reminding His true children what awaits them - fruit from the tree of life. What exactly is that fruit? We'll look into that in detail in Part Three - End Times. However, we can know for certain that any fruit promised to us by Jesus is well worth living for so as not to be embarrassed at His coming.

Letter To The Church In Smyrna

Smyrna was a coastal town built on an island but connected by an isthmus. The Christians there were suffering great persecution because they refused to acknowledge the Roman Emperor as being God.

The town's name comes from the word myrrh which is an incense taken from a tree resin. Three times in the New Testament myrrh is used in connection with Jesus. You may have guessed the first time was when Jesus was born. The wise men from the east brought gifts of gold, frankincense, and myrrh. The second time was when Jesus was on the cross. A mixture of wine and myrrh was offered to him. It's believed it was a type of pain relief. The third time was at His burial. Jesus' body was bathed in myrrh and other spices and wrapped in strips of linen. (Matt 2:11, Mk 15:23, Jn 19:39)

Myrrh is most always associated with death. Why, then, was it brought to Him at His birth? Jesus' whole mission was to die for the sins of the world. *"For God so loved the world, He gave His only begotten Son, that whosoever believeth in Him should not perish but have everlasting life"* (John 3:16, King James Version). Interestingly, there is no mention of myrrh in any Scripture concerned with Jesus after His resurrection. Why? He has conquered death forevermore. Therefore, He and all God's children are triumphant over death forevermore.

2:8, *"Write this letter to the angel of the church in Smyrna. This is the message from the One who is the First* *and the Last, who was dead but now is alive."*

This declaration from Jesus is a victorious reminder of who He is, the One who conquered death. Therefore, if He conquered, and we are in Him, then we are also conquerors. This reminds me of the passage in Romans 8:31 where Paul asks, *"If God is for us, then who can ever be against us?"* He answers his own question in verses 37-39, *"…we are more than conquerors through Him who loved us. For I am convinced that neither death nor life, neither angels nor demons, neither the present nor the future, nor any powers, neither height nor depth, nor anything else in all creation, will be able to separate us from the love of God that is in Christ Jesus our Lord"* (New International Version).

2:9, *"I know about your suffering and your poverty — but you are rich! I know the blasphemy of those opposing you. They say they are Jews, but they are not, because their synagogue belongs to Satan."*

I find the use of the word "know" comforting here. I suppose it must also have been comforting to the Christians of Smyrna, for not only did Jesus know because He is aware of their current troubles, but He knew because He, too, had experienced the greatest of suffering, physically and spiritually, when He died on the cross to pay for the sins of the world.

We can make an educated assumption here that there were those in the church who were not true Christians but were troublemakers. Jesus says outright that their true synagogue is the one of Satan, their master. People pretending to be Christians, when their desire is simply to stir up trouble in the church, has sadly been one of Satan's ploys throughout history.

In communist countries like Russia, China, and others, there are government officials feigning Christianity for the purpose of collecting information to make arrests of true Christians. Satan's infiltration in the church is nothing new.

While there were troublemakers, this was not the worst of their sufferings. The Greek word for suffering is THLIPSIS, also used for the English word tribulation. It means to crush. When Jesus spoke this word to them they could immediately identify. During this time of persecution, a common method of torture was to stretch the person out on a flat surface. A heavy stone was then placed on the person's chest, rendering it difficult to breathe. The person was asked to renounce Jesus. When they refused, more stones were placed on their chests until it became impossible to draw breath. They died an agonizing death of suffocation.

Once again, we are reminded that this word used by Jesus had to be reassuring to them. He knew about their crushing because He also had suffered an agonizing death.

Jesus then declares that in spite of their suffering and their poverty, they are rich! This reminds me of the verse in II Corinthians 8:9: *"You know the generous grace of our Lord Jesus Christ. Though He was rich, yet for your sakes He became poor, so that by His poverty He could make you rich."* Let's break this down: Though Jesus was rich - He left the rich glories of Heaven - He became poor. By His poverty - living among us and like us to die for our sins - He made us rich by giving us the promise of the glories of Heaven for eternity. Isn't that an exciting promise!

This is a promise for us today. There has always been persecution of Christians. We know the stories of Christians being fed to the lions or burned at the stake. Christians are being killed for their faith around the world even as you are reading these words. Could it come to western countries? We like to assure ourselves that in free, democratic societies, persecution of Christians would never take place. However, we need only pay attention to world news to see that nations and their leaders are making conscious decisions to turn away from godly things. They are turning their backs on Biblical standards.

As an American, I can say that when I was a child and young adult, I could never have imagined that there would be a time when killing the unborn child would be accepted as the norm. I could never have dreamed that homosexuality would have been applauded as something wonderful. I could never have dreamed that removing prayer from public places and desecrating our national flag would be okay. I could never have dreamed that in our nation's capital, acceptance of any other god in place of God the Father, God the Son, and God the Holy Spirit would become the norm. With this in mind, I encourage all true believers in Jesus Christ to be ready. It is very possible that we will individually be persecuted for our faith in Jesus and for choosing to abide in His ways. Even so, is there any encouragement? Oh yes. Read on.

2:10, *"Don't be afraid of what you are about to suffer. The devil will throw some of you into prison to test you. You will suffer for ten days. But if you remain faithful even when facing death, I will give you the crown of life."*

Upon first reading this verse you may understandably be thinking — this is encouraging? We may have all these horrible things happen to us, but don't be afraid!? Simply telling us not to be afraid is supposed to be enough to help? When we read this with human understanding alone, it's a bit ludicrous. But remember, we have the

Holy Spirit to launch us into supernatural understanding.

When we look to the Holy Spirit for strength and guidance, He reminds us that our sufferings on earth are temporary, but the promise of Heaven is eternal. We certainly don't want to sacrifice the eternal for the hope of the temporal as those who don't yet know Jesus are currently doing. Throughout God's Word there are promises that give us needed strength to stand up for Jesus no matter the earthly cost.

It's essential to our spiritual resolve to keep our eyes on Jesus and on His Word. As we are told in Psalm 119:105, *"Your Word is a lamp to guide my feet and a light for my path."* We are also reminded in Hebrews 13:5-6, *"...For God has said,*

'I will never fail you. I will never abandon you.' So we can say with confidence, 'The Lord is my helper, so I will have no fear. What can mere people do to me?" In John 16:33, Jesus says to us, "...Here on earth you will have many trials and sorrows. But take heart because I have overcome the world." We can trust our Heavenly Father completely and know for certain that when we choose to stand for the ways of Jesus, He indeed will be our everything to get us through anything. Then, when we see Him face to face, our sorrows are over, replaced with sheer joy forever. We will not be found lacking. We stand up for Jesus on earth and will not be ashamed of his coming.

Jesus continues in Revelation 2:10 to tell the church that they will suffer for ten days. I found this to be interesting and wanted to know more. It couldn't be a literal ten days because the persecution in Smyrna and among the other churches went on for years. In my Biblical research and in reading the thoughts of other theologians, I came across comments made by Dr. David Jeremiah. He felt this referred to the fact that God has time in His hands. He stands outside of time and sees it all, the beginning from the end, at the same time. In other words, Dr. Jeremiah felt Jesus was encouraging them by saying the suffering may seem to last forever, but there will indeed be an end. It may be ten days, figuratively speaking, but it won't be eleven. Therefore, stand true and strong.

Jesus closes this by promising His readers that although you may face death, an eternal crown awaits you.

There will be a time when all sorrow and suffering will be gone. Joy will last for eternity.

2:11, *"Anyone with ears to hear must listen to the Spirit and understand what He is saying to the churches. Whoever is victorious will not be harmed by the second death."*

This encourages us again to go beyond human understanding; instead, take the wisdom of the Holy Spirit. The Holy Spirit will always guide us into truth and courage. The letter ends with the wonderful promise that all who are victorious, meaning all who have received Jesus as their Savior, will not experience the second death of the Great White Throne Judgment. The second death is the final, eternal separation from Christ for eternity. There will be weeping unending.

Praise the Lord, all who receive the gift of salvation offered through Jesus and are sealed for eternity to live in joy never ending!

Letter To The Church In Pergamum

Unlike Ephesus and Smyrna, which were both coastal towns, Pergamum was built high on a plateau. It began as a military fortress, but over time grew into a noted cultural and educational center.

It contained museums and theaters. The High Court was located in Pergamum. Also, it was known for its colleges and library. It had the largest library of the time, holding 200,000 volumes. The city became the Roman capital of Asia.

The name is taken from the Greek word PERGAMENTO from which we get our English word parchment. It was in this region that parchment paper was invented.

As in all the cities of this time, the people had their particular false god. Theirs was Asclepios, the god of healing. People came from afar in hopes of obtaining healing from Asclepios. As a further note of interest, over the years archeologists have discovered coins in the area with the imprint of a snake coiled on a pole. Those of you in the medical field reading this will immediately know that this symbol is the universal sign of medicine. Archeologists believe this sign originated in Pergamum. I like to take a step back even further. Remember, Satan is a deceiver. He often deceives through imitating, pretending to be light when he is darkness.

There is a story recorded in Numbers 21:4-8. The people of Israel were led by God, using Moses, towards the promised land of Canaan. They had been set free from their slavery in Egypt. All along the way God had provided food and water and protection for them. Even so, they began to complain. Their complaints were nagging and selfish, without gratitude for all God had been doing for them. Therefore, God allowed poisonous snakes to crawl throughout their camp. Many people were bitten and died. When this happened the people called out to Moses pleading with him to ask God for help.

God gave this response in Numbers 21:8-9: *"Then the Lord told him, 'Make a replica snake and attach it to a pole. All who are bitten will live if they simply look at it!' So Moses made a snake out of bronze and attached it to a pole. Then anyone who was bitten by a snake could look at the bronze snake and be healed!"* Remember here that throughout the Bible bronze is a picture of judgment. Healing comes by God's design and according to His judgment. This is the first snake on a pole having to do with healing. Satan, in Pergamum, had designed an imitation, operating in the realm of darkness in the name of the false god Asclepios.

Let's now begin looking into the letter Jesus dictated to the church in Pergamum.

2:12, *"Write this letter to the angel of the church in Pergamum. This is the message from the One with the sharp two-edged sword."*

We already know that the angel is the pastor of the church. The two-edged sword is the Word of God. The Bible is the measure by which we must ascertain truth. Any teaching against God's Word is false.

2:13, *"I know that you live in the city where Satan has his throne, yet you have remained loyal to me. You refused to deny me even when Antipas, my favorite witness, was martyred among you there in Satan's city."*

We know that all the cities to whom the seven letters were written had their false gods, so why was Pergamum called Satan's city? It could be because of its sacrificial altar to Asclepios. This altar was enormous. (When I first read the measurements I was astonished; it was 115 feet long,

110 feet wide, and 40 feet high). Antipas, God's servant in that city, was killed for his allegiance to Jesus. It is most probable that he was killed on this altar as a sacrifice to Asclepios. Therefore, Jesus refers to it as Satan's throne.

Jesus praises the believers for their own loyalty in following Jesus in spite of the death of Antipas. They knew they could be next, yet they stood firm in their faith. This pleased Jesus; nevertheless, there was something He needed to point out to them in the next verse.

2:14, *"But I have a few complaints against you. You tolerate some among you whose teaching is like that of Balaam, who showed Balak how to trip up the people of Israel. He taught* *them to sin by eating food offered to idols and by committing sexual sin."*

When first reading this I was drawn to the word "few." It is the Greek word OLIGO which indeed means little in number, not many. In that case, we may wonder, why even mention it? Never forget that any sin, whether we consider it little or large, poses a seriousness that needs to be dealt with swiftly. Left to linger, sin grows and destroys. As the Apostle Paul wrote, *"...a little yeast spreads through the whole batch of dough"* (Galatians 5:9). Jesus, of course, fully understands that unchecked sin will hurt us. He loves us too much to ignore even a few things.

So, what was the sin the believers were tolerating, pretending it didn't really matter? Jesus uses the example of Balaam. The story is recorded in Numbers 21-24. To summarize, the children of Israel were now getting close to the time they would enter the promised land. In fact, a few skirmishes with the inhabitants of Canaan had already taken place with the Israelites winning each time. The Midianites and the Moabites were very aware that the children of Israel were being blessed by God. Therefore, normally enemies themselves, the Midianites and the Moabites decided to join forces. They elected a king to lead them whose name was Balak.

Balak was aware that Balaam was a prophet of God. He went to Balaam and asked him to curse Israel. We soon learn that Balaam was weak; nonetheless, he did consult God on the matter. God emphatically told Balaam he was not to curse Israel. Three times Balak asked Balaam to curse Israel, three times Balaam asked God, and three times God said no. To give due credit to Balaam, he stood by God's instruction and informed Balak that he could not curse Israel. In fact, we read in Numbers 24:25, *"Then Balaam left and returned home, and Balak also went on his way."* It's easy here to think that's the end of the story. Sadly, it is not.

Let's fast forward and read Numbers 31:16: *"These are the very ones who followed **Balaam's advice** and caused the people of Israel to rebel against the Lord at **Mount Peor"*** (emphases added). What? We thought Balaam left the scene, but we discover a terrible occurrence. Let's go back now and read Numbers 25:1-3, *"While the Israelites were camped at Acacia Grove, some of the men defiled* *themselves by having sexual relations with local Moabite women. These women invited them to attend sacrifices to their gods, so the Israelites feasted with them and worshipped the gods of Moab. In this way, Israel joined in the worship of* **Baal of Peor** (emphasis added), *causing the Lord's anger to blaze against His people."* As astonishing as this is, it is even more so to realize it was Balaam who arranged this temptation to sexual sin and worship of Baal of Peor.

Why did Balaam do this? When Balak first came to Balaam asking him to curse Israel, Balak offered Balaam a great reward. Upon refusing to curse Israel, Balaam, of course, forfeited his reward. However, we see that Balaam thought of another way to gain the spoils. He revealed to Balak how to tempt the Israelites, causing them to sin against God and resulting in God Himself bringing destruction upon those who partook in this sin. How cunning. How deceptive and cruel.

Sin never brings good rewards. Jesus is reminding the church at Pergamum of this fact by bringing up the story of Balaam. Giving in to any sin, even those we consider small, is never a good thing. Sin always results in loss, be it loss of joy and peace, loss of healthy relationship with others, or broken fellowship with God.

Reading the warning of Jesus to the church in Pergamum, we have to ask ourselves if we are guilty of compromise or turning a blind eye to sin. Look at the world in which we live. There was a time when sinful acts were kept secret. Now they are flaunted.

I was a child in the 1960s, a teenager in the 1970s. I remember that even non-Christians knew that homosexuality was wrong, that extra-marital affairs were wrong, that murdering unborn children was wrong. Everyone understood it. Now? Those things are applauded by the world as being wonderful because now we accept everyone as they are, without judging. The claim is that the human race is getting better.

The question for every Christian must be: what is the church doing about it? Do we individually and collectively stand against sin, voicing God's Word in these matters? Or, like the church in Pergamum, do we turn a blind eye?

I have the pleasure of speaking in many churches of varying denominations around the world. In the past 20 years I have seen more and more sin creeping into the church, which is accepted because "everyone is doing it." Having children outside of marriage is accepted as the norm. I have seen weddings where the couple, finally deciding to marry after years of living together, have their children as the ring bearers and flower children. It's all accepted because "everyone is doing it." There are churches now offering blessings on same sex relationships because "everyone is doing it."

Watch the world news. How many Christians do you see today openly standing up against sin? Some. A few. Where are the others? Each of us must heed the warning of Jesus to measure everything by God's Sword, His Word, and then stand up for it. We must never be guilty of compromising God's Word.

Anita Bryant is an American singer I remember from my youth. Many of you my age may recall the public stand she took against homosexuality. She was harassed terribly, but she stood strong. She was shouted at, called names, spit on, and even had some of her concerts cancelled. Her rewards will be great at the Judgment Seat. She suffered on earth but will be rewarded for eternity.

2:15-16, *"In a similar way, you have some Nicolaitans among you who follow the same teaching. Repent of your sin, or I will come to you* *suddenly and fight against them with the sword of my mouth."*

The Nicolaitans were a cult replete with false teachings distorting the Word of God. Jesus exhorts the church to repent of their compromise, of their turning blind eyes to sin. Remember, repenting isn't just saying you're sorry, but it means to turn away from sin with a desire not to continue in it. Jesus tells them that if they do not repent, He will come suddenly and fight with the sword of His mouth. What does this mean?

Coming suddenly refers to His return at The Rapture. Then the Judgment Seat of Christ takes place when rewards are given. If we do not repent, we have no rewards and can't argue our case because Jesus *"will fight with the sword of His mouth."* In other words, you and I will be without excuse. Our defense will not stand against the Word of God. Let us repent of sin on a daily basis. Speedy repentance is a sign of a mature Christian. Then, at the trumpet sound, we will not be embarrassed at His sudden arrival.

2:17, *"Anyone with ears to hear must listen to the Spirit and understand what He is saying to the churches. To everyone who is victorious I will give some of the manna that has been hidden away in heaven. And I will give to each one a white stone, and on the stone will be engraved a new name that no one understands except the One who receives it."*

First, a reminder that we need the guidance of the Holy Spirit to teach us, leading us into truth as we study

God's Word. The manna reminds us of how God provided for the children of Israel as He led them to the promised land. He is leading us today to the promised heaven and He provides all we need to live in peace along the way no matter the difficulties that challenge us.

The believers at Pergamum would have understood perfectly the mention of the white stone. Remember, this city housed the High Court. When someone was accused and brought to the court, the judge would listen to the lawyers present their arguments. Then he would pronounce his judgment. He did this by way of a stone.

At the end of the trial, the judge would hand a small box to the defendant who would open the box to see what color of stone was inside. A black stone meant conviction. A white stone meant acquittal. How relieved the person would be to find a white stone.

This is the same for every believer in Christ. We are all guilty of sin; however, because Jesus paid the penalty, we are counted as innocent. We are granted a white stone.

Also, during this time, when people received invitations to banquets, it was the tradition to get your invitation by way of a white stone with your name engraved on it. Without the stone with your name, you would not be granted entrance. You and I are granted entrance to Heaven by way of our names written in the Book of Life. There is no other way to gain entrance but through Jesus Christ who then gives us each a new name for eternity.

This reminds me of the verse in Matthew 7:13-14, *"You can enter God's Kingdom only through the narrow gate. The highway to hell is broad, and its gate is wide for the many who choose that way. But the gateway to life is very narrow and the road is difficult, and only a few ever find it."*

Letter To The Church In Thyatira

Thyatira was the smallest of the seven cities but still a leader in manufacturing. Known in this area for its purple dyes and for making objects of bronze, it also had a large and powerful Trade Guild. It was so powerful that one could not do business in this city without being a member of the Guild.

2:18, *"Write this letter to the angel of the church in Thyatira. This is the message from the Son of God, whose eyes are like flames of fire, whose feet are like polished bronze."*

Once again, we know that the angel is the pastor. Jesus particularly reminds this church that He is the One with eyes like fire, meaning He sees all, and He is the One with feet like bronze, meaning He is the ultimate judge.

2:19, *"I know all the things you do. I have seen your love, your faith, your s e r v i c e , a n d y o u r p a t i e n t endurance. And I can see your constant improvement in all these things."*

Jesus begins by praising them for the things they are doing correctly. He assures them that He sees their sincerity in love, service, and patient endurance. He knows they want to do the right things, and indeed in some areas they are improving.

2:20-21, *"But I have this complaint against you. You are permitting that woman — that Jezebel who calls herself a prophet — to lead my servants astray. She teaches them to* *commit sexual sin and to eat food offered to idols. I gave her time to repent, but she does not want to turn from her immorality."*

We know from the Old Testament that there was a woman, an evil queen, named Jezebel. There are theologians who believe that the Jezebel of Thyatira was a literal woman, while others believe she is a reference to the demonic stronghold of sexual sin that had taken hold. In my own research I have concluded her to be the latter. It isn't categorically defined, but I have reached this conclusion because of the Trade Guilds.

It was unlawful in Thyatira to conduct business without being a member of the Trade Guild. However, for the Christian, this was problematic. You see, as a part of their business meetings, they would also share a meal together. That in itself isn't a bad thing; however, what it represented was terrible. The feast was conducted as a part of idol worship and also included sexual acts with temple prostitutes.

We now readily see why Jesus addresses this sin, instructing the church to have no part in it. Sadly, as we read in verse 21, many were refusing to repent. They were turning a blind eye. They were scared. How would they make a living if they declined membership in the Trade Guild?

We have to stop here and examine our own hearts. This was a letter given to the church 2000 years ago, and yet, like all the letters in Revelation, it is applicable to the Church today. We must take an honest look into the behavior and attitudes of our local churches and of our own personal walks with God.

Let's look at the modern Church. I'm speaking from personal observation now as I have watched the attitudes of Satan creep unaware into the Church. The churches of today mean well, just as the church in Thyatira, but many are deceived. For example, I shared that when I was a child in the '60s and '70s, Christians and non-Christians alike believed that marriage was between one man and one woman. They also believed that the correct order of events was to fall in love, get married, then live together and have children. Not so today.

Today it is accepted in the world to live together if you love each other, and have children when you like, whether married or not. What does it matter? Astonishingly, this same acceptance has crept into many churches, with pastors and mature Christians turning blind eyes in the name of "being accepting."

A few years ago I learned that a Sunday School teacher was currently unmarried but living with her boyfriend. Privately I asked the pastor about it. I wondered if perhaps he had been unaware; but no, he knew the situation. He told me, "We just want to love them into the Kingdom." He meant well, but he was deceived. Jesus is very clear that we are to lead others to freedom in Christ, which means that they become free of the sin that has become a stronghold in their lives. If no one tells them, they ignorantly live in sin which keeps them from running over with God's blessings that they would otherwise obtain. Blatantly turning a blind eye to someone's transgression is never helpful to the person trapped in that sin.

It was no mistake that Jesus began this letter by reminding the people of Thyatira that He has eyes of fire that sees all and feet of bronze that judge all. While Pergamum was guilty of compromise, Thyatira had gone the next step - embracing evil practices that were and are blatantly against God's Word. They made the mistake of listening to the deceiving lies of the enemy. "How will you make a living?" Satan put the question to them, "Why, you have a responsibility to care for your family. Therefore, you must take part." They considered the advice which sounded right to them, and the predicament seemed insurmountable; therefore, they gave in. This same attitude prevails in the Church today because Satan lies now as he has always lied. Remember, he will make anything sound reasonable to keep you from walking in the precepts of God.

I want to mention something about Lydia here. The story of Lydia is told in Acts 16. The Apostle Paul travelled to Philippi, Greece. He heard about a group of people that gathered by the river to pray on the Sabbath. Verse 14 tells us that one of the group was *"Lydia from Thyatira, a merchant of expensive purple cloth, who worshipped God. As she listened to us, the Lord opened her heart, and she accepted what Paul was saying."* Isn't this interesting, considering what we know about Thyatira?

Remember, a merchant could not do business without being a member of the Trade Guild. The story in Acts lets us know that Lydia and her family worshiped God. Until Paul explained Jesus as the Messiah they didn't know about Him. Even so, they had worshipped God. Is that why Lydia and her family left Thyatira and moved to Greece? The Scripture doesn't tell us, but an educated guess makes me believe this is a strong possibility. Lydia and her family refused to compromise. Refusing to join the Trade Guild, they moved, trusting God to watch over them.

When we find our churches are compromising and even blatantly turning a blind eye to sin, it may be that the only godly option is to leave. When you are looking for a church home, pay attention to how the members live. Do they desire to keep themselves pure and holy no matter the ridicule of the world, or are they trying to blend in to look more acceptable to those who are not following Christ? Are they sacrificing holiness on the altar of being accepting?

I visited one church that had changed their sanctuary to look like a coffee shop, "To help those who aren't Christians to feel more comfortable to come inside," a pastor told me. I could see the pastor meant well, but he had been deceived. Read what Jesus said in John 17:14-16 as He prayed to His Father about those who were following Him, *"I have given them Your Word. And the world hates them because they do not belong to the world, just as I do not belong to the world. I'm not asking You to take them out of the world, but to keep them safe from the evil one. They do not belong to this world any more than I do."*

Jesus and His followers were often treated badly because they did not live as the world lived. We are not to live as the world lives. We live in the world but we are not a part of the world's ethos. We have a higher calling to holiness.

To be sure, there is nothing wrong at all with making the church look like a coffee shop. The problem came when people came and left there without ever hearing that Jesus loves them, wants to forgive their every sin, and free them to live an abundant life on earth with the promise of a perfect life for eternity. I have heard people tell me that they just want to be friendly and not offend people with symbols of the cross. Let us never forget I Corinthians 1:18: *"The message of the cross is foolishness to those who are headed for destruction! But we who are being saved know it is the very power of God."*

This brings to mind the passage in Colossians 4:2-6, *"Devote yourselves to prayer with an alert mind and a thankful heart. Pray for us, too, that God will give us many opportunities to speak about His mysterious plan concerning Christ. That is why I am here in chains. Pray that I will proclaim this message as clearly as I should.* ***Live wisely among those who are not believers, and make the most of every opportunity*** (emphasis added). *Let your conversation be gracious and attractive so that you will have the right response for everyone."* Paul knew the value of making the most of the time because no one knows what tomorrow may bring. Therefore, by all means serve coffee in your churches, but never in place of sharing what happened on the cross!

Every human is born with a void that longs to be filled. This void calls out for meaning in life, for 'purpose' rather than just breathing and eating, sleeping and waking. People try all sorts of things in their quest for inner peace and meaning to life. They may try drugs, or sex, or making money, or climbing the ladder to success and prestige. They may enjoy the journey at first, but there comes a moment when they realize they are not satisfied. Why? Those of us who know Jesus have discovered that only He satisfies our every longing. Only He gives peace that passes all comprehension. Only He gives courage and strength when cowardice and weakness might be the norm. Jesus is the only way to joyful, peaceful living to the fullest.

Suppose there comes a time when someone, fed up with their own life, considers that maybe they will go to church. "Perhaps I'll try God," they tell themself. So, they leave the coffee shop of the world, only to step inside the church building to find more of the same. Everyone is friendly and accepting of them just the way they are, but no one tells them they don't have to stay that way. They have come with a void that needs to be filled with the truth of II Corinthians 5:17, *"If anyone is in Christ, he is a new creation. Old things have passed away; behold, all things are become new"* (New King James Version).

Beware the church that sacrifices the Good News of Jesus on the altar of being accepting. Friendship evangelism works in the Kingdom of God as long as there is balance of friendship and evangelism; never more friendship and less evangelism.

Personally, I prefer methods of friendship evangelism. The ministries I have been involved in share the Gospel largely through making friends first. Those of you who know about the outreach in Central Asia where I've been involved for 30 years, are aware that we feed the homeless, clothe the orphans, supply food and medicines to the homebound, and spend time with those in nursing homes. It has been a tremendous joy to make friends over a meal, but the meal never ends without the dinner guests also hearing about the Bread of Life. I encourage everyone everywhere to seize every moment to share Jesus because the time of His return is near. Never forget that Satan's tactics are shrewd. He always lies with the greatest of deceptive practices. Beware distortion of Scripture. <u>Beware the tragic deception of "nice" instead of Jesus.</u>

2:22-23, *"Therefore, I will throw her on a bed of suffering, and those who commit adultery with her will suffer greatly unless they repent and turn away from her evil deeds. I will strike her children dead. Then all the churches will know that I am the One who searches out the thoughts and intentions of every person. And I will give to each one whatever you deserve."*

These two verses have rendered much theological discussion as to whether this is written figuratively or literally. I prefer just to say this: whether figurative or literal, it is most certainly cautionary. God takes holiness seriously. He takes false teaching of His Word seriously. He takes flippant attitudes of not walking in His precepts seriously. Throughout Scripture He warns His children to beware of false teachers. It seems incredible, as we read about Thyatira, their acceptance of obvious sin. We tell ourselves that we would never worship false gods and partake in sexual practices with prostitutes. We find ourselves wondering with open mouths how the church there could have become so deceived and weak.

The church today may have these thoughts about Thyatira while at the same time they are seeking to "reinvent themselves." Have you come across that mode of thinking? Another thought today is how to make the church more "relevant." There are books written on these topics. When I hear a church leader contemplating how to make their church "more relevant," the question comes to me, when did Jesus become irrelevant?

Jesus is the same today as He was yesterday, and He will be the same tomorrow. His message does not change. His call to holiness does not change. When people are sick of their lives and want something more, they don't come to church hoping to find the same things their empty lives already provide. They want something different. They want something new. They want something that will give them purpose. They don't know it when they walk in the door, but before they exit, they need to know they want Jesus.

They don't need a building that has removed the cross from its decor so as not to make someone feel uncomfortable.   They need to know the cross is an offense in this world, but those coming to it will be changed for an eternity outside of this world. They don't need a building where the word sin is never mentioned because it doesn't sound nice.   They need to know that sin is more than not nice, it's deadly; but through Jesus alone forgiveness of any sin can be found.

I fear there are churches today, rightly and lovingly seeking to be relevant, who instead, have been deceived by Satan, becoming irrelevant. These churches may gain a higher attendance.   The finances may grow, enabling them to serve their community in practical ways. They may build huge auditoriums. However, the only question in the midst of all this is: Are lives being added to the Kingdom of God? Is repentance of sin taught as a necessity for joyful living in Jesus? Is the Word of God honored in all areas of life? Positive answers to these questions define the relevant church.

2:24-28, *"But I also have a message for the rest of you in Thyatira who have not followed this false teaching (deeper truths as they call them — depths of Satan, actually). I will ask nothing more of you except that you hold tightly to what you have until I come. To all who are victorious, who obey me to the very end, to them I will give authority over all the nations. They will rule the nations* *with an iron rod and smash them like clay pots. They will have the same authority I received from my Father, and I will also give them the morning star."*

Jesus praises them for not following Satan's deception. He further encourages them by saying He will ask nothing more but to continue holding those truths — tightly! It is through God's Word that we learn to discern between truth and a lie. II Timothy 2:15-16 tells us, *"Work hard so you can present yourself to God and receive His approval. Be a good worker, one that does not need to be ashamed and who correctly explains the Word of truth. Avoid foolish talk that only leads to more foolish behavior."* Satan and his demonic forces never tire of deception. We, too, must never tire of seeking truth in

God's Word. We must work hard discovering the ways of God. Then, we will never be ashamed before God. We will have His approval, and at the time of the Judgment Seat we will receive rewards.

This passage in Timothy further instructs us not to waste time in foolish arguments. When you know God's Word, and you come across someone who wants to distort it, state its truth and then move on. Foolish argument, God tells us, can only lead to godless behavior. Stay away from senseless debate. No need to resort to anger. Step away.

In Revelation 26-28 we have the exciting reminder that after the Tribulation, during the Millennial Reign of Christ, every Christian will be given a position of authority and responsibility. There is a more detailed explanation in Part Three of this book.

I love the reference in verse 28 to the "morning star." Jesus refers to Himself here. Did you know that Venus is called the morning star? Why? Because it shines its very brightest just before daybreak. It signals that darkness is fading and the day is breaking. This is Jesus. When we come to Him, He makes us a new creation. He calls us out of darkness into His wonderful light (I Peter 2:9).

2:29, *"Anyone with ears to hear must listen to the Spirit and understand what He is saying to the churches."*

Here Jesus reminds us that we must not listen with human understanding alone but with the discernment of the Holy Spirit. It is the Spirit who guides us into truth and reveals the enemy's deception.

Letter To The Church In Sardis

Unlike the other cities that were built on the coast or the plains, Sardis was built on a plateau. It began as a fortress, a citadel overlooking the plains surrounding it. Like the other cities, it also had its false god. The citizens of Sardis worshipped Artemis, the Greek goddess of the hunt. At first I thought this a bit strange as Sardis was known for mining gold and precious jewels, especially the fire opal. However, upon further reflection I could see they would sadly look to Artemis to give them luck in their hunt in the mines.

Archeologists have discovered coins in the area and believe that it was here that the coin was invented. Possibly this came about because of the precious metals that were mined.

Coins for monetary trade would have been a useful item to use in business dealings.

3:1, *"Write this letter to the angel of the church in Sardis. This is the message from the One who has the sevenfold Spirit of God and the seven stars: 'I know all the things you do, and that you have a reputation for being alive — but you are dead'..."*

Jesus instructs this letter to be written to the pastor. He proclaims this letter is from the One who possesses all the godly characteristics. We first referenced this in the first chapter of Revelation citing Isaiah 11:2: *"And the Spirit of the Lord will rest on Him — the Spirit of wisdom and understanding, the Spirit of counsel and might, the Spirit of knowledge and of the fear of the Lord."* Along with possessing these godly characteristics, Jesus also assures them that He holds the seven stars or churches. It's comforting to know He holds us all in His hands and nothing can pry open the fingers of God to snatch us out! What a safe place to be!

Next Jesus jumps right in with hard truth. He tells them He is aware of their reputation for being alive — but severely proclaims they are dead. This may seem confusing upon first reading, but not so baffling after further reflection.

Our reputation is formed by outward appearances. Doing good works and speaking kind words builds a reputation that is admired. Isn't that a good thing, we may say? After all, to be thought of in high regard is surely something to be desired. Indeed, but not if that is the whole reason we perform good works.

Jesus is going right to the crux of the matter. He is cutting through the outward works, exposing the inward heart. He is challenging them in a matter of spiritual life or death. Jesus could clearly see that some in the church of Sardis had heard the Good News of Jesus. They knew that Jesus died to save us all from our sins. They also knew that the only way to eternal life in heaven is through Jesus alone. However, having heard the Good News, they considered it, came close to receiving Jesus as Savior — but did not receive Him. Instead, they got involved in the church doing good works. Perhaps they helped serve the poor, or took part in some other community service in the name of the church. Nevertheless, Jesus knew they weren't doing anything in His name because they weren't part of Him. They had never actually asked Jesus to forgive them and become Lord of their lives.

This reminds me of one of the saddest portions of Scripture, Matthew 7:21-23. *"Not everyone calling out to me, 'Lord! Lord!' will enter the Kingdom of Heaven. Only those who actually do the will of my Father in heaven will enter. On judgment day many will say to me, 'Lord! Lord! We prophesied in Your name and cast out demons in Your name and performed many miracles in Your name.' But I will reply, 'I never knew you. Get away from me, you who break God's laws.'"*

What exactly does it mean, *"only those who actually do the will of my Father in heaven will enter,"* and *"get away you who break God's laws?"* What is the will of the Father? What is His law? His will, written as law, Is this: there is no amount of good work that one can do to earn entrance into heaven. It is only through the shed blood of His Son, Jesus. He is the only way through whom we may be saved (John 14:6). We know that God loved the world so much, as the Scripture tells us in John 3:16, that He gave His Son to die for our sins. Jesus longs for each person to receive His gift of salvation. Therefore, to the church in Sardis, and to the church today, He writes a severe rebuke of warning.

3:2, *"Wake up! Strengthen what little remains, for even what is left is almost* dead. I find that your actions do not meet the requirements of my God."

Jesus shouts to bring about a shocking wake up call. Individuals in the church have heard the truth. They know what is required to go to heaven. They refuse to ask God's forgiveness of their sins and are nearly asleep in their complacency, so He shouts to "Wake up!"

3:3, "Go back to what you heard and believed at first; hold to it firmly. Repent and turn to me again. If you don't wake up, I will come to you suddenly, as unexpected as a thief."

Here Jesus makes reference to The Rapture, which will come unexpectedly. Remember, these letters are written to prepare the church to be ready and not ashamed at His coming. Jesus encourages them to consider again the truth of the Gospel they heard earlier, but this time actually receive the gift of salvation. Not to merely acknowledge it's a good thing, but to repent before God, receive His forgiveness, and be counted as one of His children. Do it, He urges them, before The Rapture takes place and they are then left behind to face unimaginable tribulation.

3:4-5, *"Yet there are some in the church in Sardis who have not soiled their clothes with evil. They will walk with me in white, for they are worthy. All who are victorious will be clothed in white. I will never erase their names from the Book of Life, but I will announce before my Father and His angels that they are mine."*

To those in the church who have received His gift of salvation, Jesus tells them they will walk in white clothing, symbolizing purity because all who know Him are washed clean by His precious blood. He says we are worthy, and what makes us worthy? Nothing we have done, but all that Jesus has done on the cross.

To everyone who receives Jesus, their names are never erased from the book of Life. Some have made the mistake of thinking that when we ask forgiveness and invite Jesus into our lives, that our name is added to the Book of Life. No, at the moment of conception, that person's name is written in the Book of Life. It would only be upon final rejection of Christ that the name is erased. When we are one by one presented to the Father, imagine the excitement as we hear

Jesus say, "This one is mine!" - all because our names will never be erased from the Book of Life.

3:6, *"Anyone with ears to hear must listen to the Spirit and understand what He is saying to the churches."*

Jesus always reminds us that it is the Holy Spirit within us who teaches us and guides us into all truth. When we need clarity, all we have to do is ask the Holy Spirit to open our ears of understanding and bless us with wisdom.

Letter To The Church In Philadelphia

Philadelphia was located at the bottom of a mountain near the river Cogamus. The plains around the city were fertile making it possible to grow an abundance of grapes. It is no surprise, therefore, that the region was known for its fine wines. Philadelphia had been known by several names: Dacapolis, Flavia, and Little Athens. This was a result of earthquake destruction. The city was left in ruins, rebuilt, and then renamed. It was called Little Athens no doubt because, like Athens, it boasted many pagan temples to both Roman and Greek gods and goddesses. There were many pagan festivals, sexual promiscuity with temple prostitutes, and sacrifices to the various false gods in Philadelphia.

3:7, *"Write this letter to the angel of the church in Philadelphia. This is the message from the One who is holy and true, the One who has the key of David. What He opens, no one can close; and what He closes, no one can open."*

The introduction, as in every letter, is to the pastor of the church. Jesus points out that He is the One who is perfect holiness and truth, and has the Key of David. What is this Key of David?

It's only mentioned twice in Scripture, the first being in Isaiah 22:22, *"I will give him the key to the house of David — the highest position in the royal court. When he opens doors, no one will be able to close them; when he closes doors, no one will be able to open them."* This Old Testament passage is a reference to Eliakim, Finance Minister to King Hezekiah. The key was a symbol of his authority. No one could enter the Treasury or the King's Offices without the permission of the Finance Minister.   If he commanded an entrance closed, it was closed and vice versa.

We find the second reference to the Key of David in the above verse in Revelation. Jesus is reminding the citizens of Philadelphia of His authority. No one will enter His Father's chambers or gain entrance into the riches of heaven without His permission. We know that permission is only granted to those washed in the blood of the Lamb. Therefore, if He opens the entrance of Heaven for those washed in His blood, no one can close it. Alternatively, if one's name is not written in the Book of Life, no amount of excuses in the world can gain one's entrance to Heaven.

Another thought that can be taken from this Scripture concerns opportunities. God has a plan for you and He has a plan for me. In His plans He may design a path that leads you to go through a particular door. Let's say you refuse. Will the opportunity be lost because of your refusal? Absolutely not, because what He opens no man can close. If you or I refuse to seize an opportunity that God gives us, He will simply choose someone else to go through the door.

Many of you are familiar with my personal testimony concerning God sending me to Central Asia in 1991 as recorded in my book <u>With Wings Like An Eagle.</u> The first year there was particularly difficult.   I was getting used to a new culture, language, work ethic, and food rations! Winters were unbelievably cold. The heating in my apartment didn't work well. If I wanted milk, I had to wake up at 5:00am, walk in the snow for a block, and stand in a line to wait for a man in a truck to put a hose into my glass jar and fill it with unpasteurized milk. Back at home I would bring the milk to a low boil to kill bacteria and remove whatever floated to the top, like bits of straw. This was not fun.

I considered leaving. The Holy Spirit spoke loudly that I was to stay put. In spite of great misery I stayed. However, obedience brought blessing. Through all these years I've had the joy of watching God do amazing things in that part of the world. I could have refused to go through the open door. God would never close the door He opened. If I turned away, He would have brought someone else. I would have missed such tremendous joy.

When God gives you an opportunity, I encourage you, never attempt to close the door and never refuse to go through it. The way may be hard and scary, but the results will be joy immeasurable. Remember, obedience always brings blessings. Also, you will never walk alone because where our Lord leads us, He always goes with us.

3:8, *"I know all the things you do, and I have opened a door for you that no one can close. You have little strength, yet you obeyed my word and did not deny me."*

Jesus continues with the theme of opportunity. He assures them that He knows all they are doing. They have seized the opportunity. They are weak, strength fading, but they keep pressing forward. This reminds me of something the Apostle Paul said in II Corinthians 12.

Paul had an affliction that troubled him to the point he asked God to remove it. Three times Paul asked God and three times God denied the request, along with the reminder that God's power works best in weakness. This encouraged Paul because he understood that when he is weak, then God's power shines through. That's why Paul goes on to say in II Corinthians 12:10, "...*I take pleasure in my weaknesses, and in the insults, hardships, persecutions, and troubles that I suffer for Christ. For when I am weak, then I am strong."*

This is a favorite verse of mine and no doubt of many of you, too. What a tremendous encouragement that there is no difficulty so great that God's strength can be hindered. Impossible! When God's strength becomes our strength, then no discouragement can destroy us.

3:9, *"Look, I will force those who belong to Satan's synagogue — those liars who say they are Jews but are not — to come and bow down at your feet. They will acknowledge that you are the ones I love."*

We are all aware that at times there are those who make a pretense of Christianity for no other reason than greed or hatred. By way of example, we've all seen so called ministers who are obviously traveling this road for money. I assure you that most ministers are not corrupt, but the few that are participate in Satan's deceit. Also, some people pretend to be Christians just to make trouble. I have personally known this to happen in communist countries. I have met pastors in Russia and China who told me of "informers" in their churches, planted by police officials, to report on those who attend the church. They are only there to cause trouble for followers of Jesus.

In the above verse, Jesus comforts and encourages the Christians of Philadelphia, as well as us today. Jesus knows when we are being troubled by those making a pretense of Christianity, when in reality, their mission is actually Satan's. To those suffering in this manner, Jesus gives assurance that there will come a time when those who have sought to do evil to us will honor us. All who refuse Jesus will bow before Him and honor us in recognition that we are the ones Jesus loves.

3:10, *"Because you have obeyed my command to persevere, I will protect you from the great time of testing that will come upon the whole world to test those who belong to this world."*

This is a reference to the time of Tribulation that will begin immediately following The Rapture. Jesus encourages us all that if we have accepted Him by the time of The Rapture, then of a certainty, we will be taken away before Tribulation begins.

3:11, *"I am coming soon. Hold on to what you have, so that no one will take away your crown."*

This is a reference to The Judgment Seat of Christ, that time when Christians will receive rewards for being steadfast in the ways of Jesus. We don't want to be saved by the skin of our teeth, receiving no rewards, having nothing to give back to Jesus. What a sadness that would be.

3:12, *"All who are victorious will become pillars in the Temple of my God, and they will never have to leave it. And I will write on them the name of my God, and they will be citizens in the City of my God — the new Jerusalem that comes down from heaven from my God. And I will also write on them my new name."*

I feel such excitement when I read this verse. First, let's talk about those pillars. The people of Philadelphia would have precisely understood the illustration Jesus was making. Since the area was known for earthquakes, the pillars which adorned prominent buildings were built on beds of charcoal covered in wool fleece. Each pillar was then connected together by metal clasps. This was a remarkable architectural design for the time. The coal and wool fleece acted as a cushion, helping to keep the pillars upright in the midst of earth's tremors. When you visit this part of the world today, you will find many ruins of long ago cities. Interestingly, among the rubble, the pillars are most often intact. Now you know why.

Jesus was telling them that because they remain true to Jesus, they will not be toppled over by any temptation or ploy of Satan. No, they will remain tall and strong because they are grounded, or cushioned, on the Word of God. God's Word never fails. Jesus encourages them further by reminding them that their citizenship for eternity is in Heaven. They will be permanent residents of the City of God. In Part Three, we will discuss different aspects of Heaven in greater detail.

In the City of God we will also be given a new name from Jesus. When I first read this I had a moment of sadness. I like my name, Vickie. Why would it have to be changed? Perhaps you've had the same thought. Even so, I quickly concluded that if the name is from Jesus, it has to be good. We will not be disappointed with our new name.

3:13, *"Anyone with ears to hear must listen to the Spirit and understand what He is saying to the churches."*

Once again, Jesus implores His followers to seek the guidance of the Holy Spirit in all their ways and through all their days. Understanding the teaching and instruction of Jesus only comes by way of the Holy Spirit.

Letter To The Church In Laodicea

Laodicea was located along the river Lycus. For this reason the city became a major trade route. Boats would arrive day and night, while across the plains camel caravans would bring wares to sell, then purchase items the city had to offer.

Laodicea was particularly known for its black wool. They had factories that would weave carpets and make garments from this luxurious wool. It was a sought after item, and it was prestigious to own anything made from Laodicean black wool. Also well known was the city's medical center for ophthalmology. Specifically, the medical center had invented an eye ointment used to treat severe infections which often restored or improved sight. People would come from far away to receive this eye treatment. Due to its trade and medical center, Laodicea was rich in commerce and in the arts. It boasted beautiful monuments, parks, banks, and markets, including an ornate Temple to Zeus, king of the Greek gods.

3:14, *"Write this letter to the angel of the church in Laodicea. This is the message from the One who is the Amen — the faithful and true witness, the beginning of God's new creation."*

As He dictates this letter to the pastor, Jesus proclaims that He alone is faithful and true, the witness of God's new creation. Amen means to agree. He agrees with His Father and with the Holy Spirit that He is all of the above. What is the new creation? We find the answer in II Corinthians 5:17:

"Therefore, if any man be in Christ he is a new creation. Old things are passed away; behold, all things are become new" (King James Version). The new creation is each <u>one</u> of us who has received Jesus as Savior.

3:15-16, *"I know all the things that you do, that you are neither hot nor cold. I wish that you were one or the other! But since you are like lukewarm water, neither hot nor cold, I will spit you out of my mouth!"*

Once again Jesus makes the point that nothing can be hidden from Him. He knows the intent of our hearts and He knows why we do what we do. He appeals here to what the people will particularly understand, being Laodiceans.

Remember, they are renowned for their medical center. One of the treatments for nausea was to sip lukewarm water. It was believed that doing so would make the person vomit, thereby, begin to feel better. Only a sick person would drink lukewarm water. A healthy person would drink steaming hot tea or coffee or cold drinks like lemon and other fruit juices.

Therefore, the church would have understood perfectly what Jesus was saying to them. Their compromising - one day standing strong in things godly, the next day flirting with sin - made them lukewarm and made Jesus want to vomit. That's why He proclaims, rather severely, that He will spit them out of His mouth!

These words, *"I will spit you out of my mouth,"* have made some quake in fear, thinking this may be a reference to losing one's salvation. Not so! Once we are a child of God, we are always a child of God, sealed until the day of redemption. If ever you doubt, read Ephesians 4:30, *"And do not bring sorrow to God's Holy Spirit by the way you live. Remember, he has identified you as His own,* **guaranteeing** (emphasis added) *that you will be saved on the day of redemption."*

To properly understand what Jesus is telling them, we must use our spiritual deep sea diving tools to bring the treasures of this verse to the surface of our understanding. Let's dissect the phrase "I will." Jesus said, *"I will spit you out of my mouth."* First, the Greek word for "will" is ME'LLO. The literal meaning is "about to." In other words,

Jesus has been made so sick by their ungodly behavior that He is "about to" vomit! This is a warning to heed. He is exhorting them to examine their own sick hearts and make them clean through repentance.

This is not a reference to salvation, but about embarrassment and rewards. If we are living lukewarm when Jesus returns at The Rapture, we will be embarrassed and feel horrible when rewards are given and we get none! We will have nothing to lay at Jesus' feet in worship and thankfulness to Him.

3:17-18, *"You say, 'I am rich. I have everything I want. I don't need a thing!' And you don't realize that you are wretched and miserable and poor and blind and naked. So I advise you to buy gold from me — gold that has* been purified by fire. Then you will be rich. Also buy white garments from me so you will not be ashamed by your nakedness, and ointment for your eyes so you will be able to see."

Here, Jesus appeals to what He knows they can relate to because of the richness of the city. He is reminding them that they have misplaced priorities. They have become so comfortable with physical finery that they have ignored the spiritual condition of their hearts. Jesus further tells them that they are so focused on their physical appearance, that they don't realize they are miserable, blind, and naked spiritually.

Haven't you and I experienced that same state of being? We become comfortable in our everyday lives. We have a job, nice clothes, food in the pantry, and yet when we stop to think, a disturbance fills our being. That's the Holy Spirit telling us something is not right.

Jesus goes on to encourage them to buy gold. This reminds me of the passages in I Corinthians 3. In verse 11 we are reminded that Jesus is our foundation. Then Paul tells us, *"Anyone who builds on that foundation may use a variety of materials — gold, silver, jewels, wood, hay, or straw. But on the judgment day, fire will reveal what kind of work each builder has done. The fire will show if a person's work has any value. If the work survives, that builder will receive a reward. But if the work is burned up, the builder will suffer great loss. The builder will be saved, but like somebody barely escaping through a wall of flames" (vs. 12-15).* This passage clearly states that it is not our works that saves us, nor does lack of works cause us to lose salvation. It's all about rewards for how we have lived on earth. Once again, we don't want to be embarrassed when Jesus returns to take us to be with Him for eternity.

3:19-20, *"I correct and discipline everyone I love. So be diligent and turn from your indifference. Look! I stand at the door and knock. If you will hear my voice and open the door,* PTO *I will come in, and we will share a meal together as friends."*

Every good parent must discipline their children to train them in how to live godly, responsible lives. Once in a while the child must be sent to the "time out" chair. There, it is hoped they will think about their behavior, be sorry, make a decision to turn away from it, and then be restored in joyful fellowship with their parents. Our Heavenly Father does no less.

In verse 20 Jesus encourages us to open the door to Him. Most often this verse is used to hopefully lead someone into salvation. That's absolutely fine. However, in its literal sense this verse is appealing to those who are already Christians but have backslidden away from God, and who need to repent for their sin, thereby restoring intimacy with Jesus.

3:21, *"Those who are victorious will sit with me on my throne, just as I was victorious and sat with my Father on His throne."*

Oh, what a fabulous reminder of our destiny! To all who are in Christ Jesus, the glories of heaven await us - eternity in a place of no sorrow or tears, only joy and peace. It is a most wonderful promised inheritance.

3:22, *"Anyone with ears to hear must listen to the Spirit and understand what He is saying to the churches."*

In closing His letter to the seventh church, Jesus implores them, as He has in every letter, to keep their spiritual ears open. Hear what the Spirit is saying to you. Repent when reminded of sin in your life. Understand His will for you. *"Seek and you will find,"* as promised in Matthew 7:7-8.

It is not just given to us on a plate. We must physically seek.

A Summary Of Jesus' Words To The Seven Churches

Jesus greeted each church with a particular reason, addressing that church's need. He was meeting them where they lived. He was personal to their unique situation.

1. **Ephesus** - Jesus said, *"This is the message from the One who holds the seven stars and walks among the seven gold lamp stands."* Jesus appeals to their understanding of intimacy. He is intimate with them. He holds them and walks among them. He is close. They have forgotten how they felt when they first fell in love with Him. He encourages them to go back to that place, remember, and fall in love all

over again.

2. **Smyrna** - Jesus said, *"This is the message from the One who is the First and the Last, who was dead but is now alive."* The Christians in Smyrna were suffering great persecution with the promise of more to come. Jesus reminds them that He is the One who has conquered death. He did this on the cross, dying, and then rising from the dead on the third day. Since Jesus conquered death, and since we are His own, death has no hold on us. Therefore, we need not fear what happens to us on earth because we have a promised glorious future. Paul explained this wonderfully in Colossians 3:1-4, *"Since you have been raised to new life with*

Christ, set your sights on the realities of Heaven, where Christ sits at God's right hand. Think about the things of Heaven, not the things of earth. For you died to this life, and your real life is hidden with Christ in God. And when Christ, who is your life, is revealed to the whole world, you will share in all His glory."

3. **Pergamum** - *"This is the message from the One with the sharp, two-edged sword."* There has been persecution here just as in Smyrna. However, unlike the church in Smyrna who is standing strong in their faith, the Christians in Pergamum have compromised. They have tolerated wrong teaching. Jesus reminds them that everything must be measured against the

Word of God, which is the sharp two-edged sword. Every Christian must study God's Word to rightly interpret it, thereby standing true to its teaching. Remember II Timothy 2:15, *"Work hard so you can present yourself to God and receive His approval. Be a good worker, one who does not need to be ashamed and who **correctly explains the Word of Truth"** (emphasis added).

4. **Thyatira** - Jesus begins by telling them that He is *"the Son of God, whose eyes are like flames of fire, whose feet are like polished bronze."* The church has been overlooking false teaching. Lies have crept into the church and mature Christians are turning a blind eye, perhaps

in the name of "being accepting." Jesus reminds them that nothing can be hidden from Him. His eyes are like fire seeing through all excuses, revealing truth. His feet of bronze represent judgment. He will see all and He will judge all. We must take care to live our lives clean and holy. Jesus will judge the Christian, rendering rewards at the Judgment Seat of Christ. We don't want to be found lacking.

5. **Sardis** - Jesus proclaims that He is the *"One who has the sevenfold Spirit of God and He holds the seven stars."* The sevenfold Spirit of God most likely has those characteristics of God listed in Isaiah 11:2: *"And the Spirit of the Lord will rest on Him — the Spirit of wisdom and*

understanding, the Spirit of counsel and might, the Spirit of Knowledge and the fear of the Lord." Jesus knew their reputation for being alive, but informed them that measured by the characteristics of God, they were dead. In other words, they've heard the truth of salvation, they considered it, they nearly asked Jesus to forgive their sins and come into their lives — but they stopped short of actually making that commitment. They had the knowledge of Jesus, but lacked a relationship with Him. Jesus encouraged them to truly turn to Him, and become alive, living in those same godly characteristics as He lives. Then, when the trumpet sounds the arrival of The Rapture, they will be ready to meet Jesus in the air.

6. **Philadelphia** - Jesus reminds them that He is *"the One who has the Key of David, and what He opens no one can close, and what he closes, no one can open."* Jesus praises them for their steadfastness. They have come to Him in faith, knowing He alone can open the way to heaven. He alone provides opportunities to tell others about His saving grace. They have seized those glorious opportunities. Therefore, Jesus joyfully reminds them that they will not endure the time of Tribulation that comes immediately following The Rapture. This is a reminder to all who know Jesus. Be ready, the

time is near. He is coming soon!

7. **Laodicea** - In His last letter, Jesus announces that He is *"the faithful and true witness, the beginning of God's new creation."* What is God's new creation? Every person who comes to Jesus asking forgiveness of sin is made new. Since we are new, we should live in the ways of God that our now transformed lives represent. The Christians in Laodicea were lukewarm Christians. Lukewarm water was used to make an ill person vomit. Jesus is so sickened by their behavior that He wants to vomit Himself! He encourages repentance. He is knocking at the door of His wayward children's hearts. He longs for them to repent and

share again in intimacy with Him. Remember the beauty of I John 1:9, *"If we confess our sins, He is faithful and just, to forgive us our sins and to cleanse us from all unrighteousness"* (King James Version).

"And now dear children, remain in fellowship with Christ, so that when He returns, you will be full of courage and not shrink back from Him in shame" (I John 2:28).

PART THREE

End Times

The Rapture

Bible prophecy concerning the End Times is a subject that captivates most of us. There remains a mystery about all the events that are to take place. Understandably, questions and speculations whirl away in our minds.

As we begin this study, I will lay some groundwork concerning the viewpoint to which I adhere. There are some theologians that teach from a Pre-Tribulation point of view, others from Mid-Tribulation, and still others have a Post-Tribulation mindset. In other words, some believe The Rapture takes place before the Tribulation, some believe it takes place in the middle of the Tribulation, and some after the Tribulation. Those who believe The Rapture comes after the Tribulation are very often those who believe that The Rapture and the Second Coming of Christ are one and the same.

For the sake of our study I must let you know that I teach from the Pre-Tribulation belief. In my own study of Scripture I have concluded that The Rapture takes place before the Tribulation. I will, of course, be sharing the Scriptural reasons that bring me to this conclusion.

Someone asked me, what if I'm wrong? I often told my Bible College students that we must teach what we fully believe the Holy Spirit has revealed to us. Of course, I tell them, we are all continual students of God's Word. There are things I believe today that I did not believe in earlier years of my Christianity. I have grown and matured in my understanding of

God's Word. In answer to the question, what if I'm wrong?, I answer as follows: When we all get to heaven, we will be filled with perfect love. Therefore, we will not have our feelings hurt when we discover we were not right in everything. We must approach God's Word with an open mind, allowing the Holy Spirit to mold us, teach us truth, and endow us with holy understanding.

With that in mind, I will share with you, from a Pre-Tribulation teaching, thoughts concerning The Rapture. Throughout our look into End Times, I will not endeavor to point to every Biblical reference. I like to give enough information that hopefully whets your own appetite to dive deeper into God's Word, discovering His truths for yourselves.

It has often been said that the word rapture isn't even in the Bible so why are there people who believe it and teach it? That is an excellent question and an excellent place to begin. Let's start by looking at I Thessalonians 4:13-18: *"And now, dear brothers and sisters, we want you to know what will happen to the believers who have died so you will not grieve like people who have no hope. For since we believe that Jesus died and was raised to life again, we also believe that when Jesus returns, God will bring back with Him the believers who have died. We tell you this directly from the Lord: We who are still living when the Lord returns will not meet Him ahead of those who have died. For the Lord Himself will come down from heaven with a commanding shout, with the voice of the archangel, and with the trumpet call of God. First, the believers who have died will rise from their graves. Then, together with them, we who are still alive and remain on the earth will be caught up in the clouds to meet the Lord in the air. Then we will be with the Lord forever. So encourage each other with these words."*

I draw your attention to the end of verse 17 that tells us that those alive on earth *"will be caught up in the clouds."* This is one of those many times when doing some spiritual deep sea diving into God's Word, that we must use our tools. In this instance we'll use the Greek dictionary. In Greek, which is the original language in which the New Testament was written, the phrase, *"caught up"* is the word HARPAZO, pronounced HAR-PAD'-ZO. This Greek word literally means to be caught up or to be snatched up. Why, then, do Christians call this event The Rapture?

The New Testament was first translated from Greek into Latin. The Latin word for HARPAZO is RAPTURA. As the years went by and the New Testament was translated from Greek into English, the word HARPAZO was correctly translated "caught up." However, in ecclesiastical circles and discussions among the clergy and theological students, the Latin word RAPTURA came to be shortened to rapture. That is why Christians today refer to the "snatching away" or the being "caught up" as The Rapture.

Now let's take a look at something else in this passage that seems to contradict itself. In verse 14 we read that "...when Jesus returns, *God will bring back with Him the believers who* have died." Then in verse 16 we read "First, the believers who have died will rise from their graves." So, what's going on here? Jesus is bringing back the dead with Him, but the dead will rise from their graves to meet Him? Isn't that a contradiction?

Here we must remind ourselves that we are created in the image of God. He is triune: God the Father, God the Son, and God the Holy Spirit. We are also triune. For example, I am Vickie the spirit, Vickie the soul, and Vickie the body. Remember, the spirit is that part of us wherein, when invited, the Holy Spirit takes up residence and seals us for eternity. The soul is that part of us where we feel, think, and make decisions - our mind. The Body is that physical part we see when we look in the mirror.

When our body dies it decays away. The soul and spirit live on for eternity. When we die, our soul and spirit go immediately to be with the Lord. As the Scripture assures us in II Corinthians 5:8, when we are away from our body we are then at home with the Lord. Therefore, when Jesus returns to meet us in the air during The Rapture, the saved souls who have previously died, along with their spirits, will be coming with Jesus. Their renewed bodies will come out of the grave, rejoining their souls and spirits. Those of us alive on earth, in the twinkling of an eye (that's fast!), will be 'caught up in the air', receiving a new body which is incorruptible. We will then all be with Jesus, souls and spirits, housed in a new undying body.

Something else very important to notice is that at The Rapture when there is a sound like a trumpet, Christians living on earth *"will be caught up in the clouds to meet the Lord in the air"*. Why is this important to note? Because it differentiates between The Rapture and The Second Coming of Christ. In the first event, Jesus only comes as close as the clouds. At The Second Coming, Jesus sets foot on the earth. They are not the same event. The Rapture takes place first and ushers in the Tribulation. At the end of the seven year Tribulation, The Second Coming of Christ takes place and is the start of The Millennium or thousand year reign of Christ.

Do we have a date as to when The Rapture will take place? No date is given, but there are signs for the

Tribulation, and we know The Rapture precedes that event. Let's go back to I Thessalonians and read 5:1-8: *"Now concerning how and when all this will happen, dear brothers and sisters, we don't really need to write to you. For you know quite well that the day of the Lord's return will come unexpectedly, like a thief in the night. When people are saying, 'Everything is peaceful and secure,' then disaster will fall on them as suddenly as a pregnant woman's labor pains begin. And there will be no escape. But you aren't in the dark about these things, dear brothers and sisters, and you won't be surprised when the day of the Lord comes like a thief. For you are all children of the light and of the day; we don't belong to darkness and night. So be on your guard, not asleep like the others. Stay alert and be clearheaded. Night is the time when people sleep and drinkers get drunk.   But let us who love the light be clearheaded, protected by the armor of faith and love, and wearing as our helmet the confidence of our salvation."*

When the world at large is saying all is well, even with rampant sin abounding, that is a strong hint that the time of The Rapture is near. Take a look at your own country. For me, I have to look steadily at America. Currently, at the writing of this book, it is the strongest superpower in the world. God has blessed America abundantly. Our founding fathers made it clear that God, Creator of the Universe, is the only true God, and is the One God upon which our Constitution was written. For more than a century, God's principles were honored and obeyed in America.

Christianity was highly respected even by those who did not claim to be Christians. When I was a child, and then into my teens and young adulthood, businessmen and politicians wanted everyone to believe they lived by Christian principles (even if they weren't Christians) because those principles were respected. Public prayers were honored, practiced and encouraged. Prayer opened sports events and school graduations. Today prayer is not permitted in most public venues. The Ten Commandments were regularly printed on court house walls. Now they have been removed in many public establishments.

The right to life of every human being was always assumed. Now, people fight for full birth abortions citing the right of the woman to make a choice for her body. I always ask, "But what about the body of the child?" Who would have thought such mass murders would have been committed within the law? Marriage was always honored as God designed it to be, clearly between one man and one woman. Now, homosexuality is not only accepted as "normal" but is even honored, those "coming out of the closet" treated as heroes for throwing God's design onto the trash pile of degradation.

By the way, concerning this subject of homosexuality, I have met Christians who absolutely know it's wrong because God says it is, but they don't know how to explain their beliefs. Let's run on a rabbit trail here, taking a temporary detour from The Rapture study, and look into the matter of homosexuality from Scripture. It is vastly important to understand so we may give an answer to those who ask.

Genesis 1:27 reads, *"So God created human beings in His own image. In the image of God He created them."* In the next verse He tells them to *"be fruitful and multiply. Fill the earth and govern it."* In Genesis 2:24 we read *"...a man leaves his father and mother and is joined to his wife, and the two are united into one."*

That's simple enough to comprehend. I liken the understanding of this subject to an artist. Leonardo da Vinci painted the famous *Mona Lisa*, exhibited today in the Louvre Museum in Paris, France. No one who has a preference for blonds has the right to come along, paint another picture with a blond Mona Lisa, and demand it be displayed and accepted in the Louvre as a painting of equal value. That would be ludicrous. There is only one Mona Lisa created by the artist, Leonardo da Vinci.

Likewise, there is only one design for marriage and sexual relationship, designed by Creator God. No one who has a preference for same sex relationships has the right to come along and demand another design for marriage to be accepted as equal in value. That is also ludicrous. Since it's to do with living beings, it is also sinful.

Now let's look at a verse in Malachi 3:6 that reads, *"I am the Lord, and I do not change."* God, who can do anything, cannot change Himself. He is who He is. He is holy. His ways are perfect. There can be no improvement. Therefore, to attempt to change what He has already designed is an abomination to Him.

In just the last thirty years the world has vastly changed its regard for God, and it's not getting better. Acceptance of sin is fast becoming the norm. Persecution of Christians for choosing to abide by God's way is also becoming more and more acceptable.

Never forget to beware of the lying whispers of the enemy. He has been lying big time concerning both abortion and homosexuality, deceiving people into accepting the lie that there is a case for legalized murder and the distortion of God's marriage design.

These attitudes are another hint that The Rapture is drawing near. Let us look at two passages of Scripture. For the first we go to Matthew 24:37:

"*When the Son of man returns, it will be like it was in Noah's day.*" What was it like in Noah's day? Genesis 6:5 tell us, "*The Lord observed the extent of human wickedness on the earth, and He saw that everything they thought or imagined was consistently and totally evil.*" We know what happened as a result of this mass evil during the days of Noah. God sent the flood.

Looking again in Matthew 24, we read in verses 38-39: "*In those days before the flood the people were enjoying banquets and parties and weddings right up to the time Noah entered his boat. People didn't realize what was going to happen until the flood came and swept them all away. That is the way it will be when the Son of Man comes.*"

Jesus is very clear in His explanation here. When the world again becomes as it was in the days of Noah, that will be a sign that the time of The Rapture is near. Noah and his family, the only ones not practicing sin, were saved from the terrible disaster of the flood.

There are Christians who accept this as a sign of The Rapture, but they don't necessarily believe Christians will not have to go through at least some of the Tribulation. How do we know that Christians will be saved from experiencing the Tribulation? To answer that question we go back to I Thessalonians chapter 5. In verses 4-8, Paul is speaking about The Rapture, telling his readers that Jesus will come unexpectedly like a thief in the night. The next verses, 9-11 read, *"For God chose to save us through our*

Lord Jesus Christ, **not to pour out His anger upon us** (emphasis added). *Christ died for us so that, whether we are dead or alive when He returns, we can live with Him forever. So encourage each other and build each other up, just as you are already doing."* This makes it very clear that at The Rapture God will *"not pour out His anger upon us."* I find that comforting and exciting. Paul assures his readers that when Jesus returns at The Rapture, those dead and alive will go to be with Him.

Even though we are comforted to know The Rapture delivers Christians from the horrors of the Tribulation, never believe for a moment that persecution will not be experienced. Since the time of Jesus, those pledging themselves to Him have been persecuted. Persecution of Christians is rampant today in many parts of the world. The western church overall has been spared such persecution. However, with ever increasing ungodliness being displayed, be prepared to be persecuted in your stand for Jesus.

Satan works hard to cause dissension and disbelief in both the matter of The Rapture and the matter of persecution. After all, he doesn't want Christians to be strong in persecution, as killing your joy, stealing your peace, and destroying your hope is his constant goal. He wants Christians to be fearful of the End Times, not jubilant. I urge you to stand fast, keeping your eyes on the Word of truth, never on the deceptions of Satan. Do not give demons a foothold! Beware!

So we see what will happen to Christians at the moment of The Rapture, but what happens to those unsaved who have been left behind? The world will, in the twinkling of an eye, go into mass chaos such as has never been seen. Just imagine, Christians all over the earth will suddenly disappear. That means cars being driven by Christians and planes being piloted by Christians will crash. Surgeons who are Christians will disappear in the middle of surgeries. Christian teachers will disappear from their classrooms. Christian lawyers and judges will disappear from courtrooms. Every Christian everywhere, in the twinkling of an eye, will disappear. Can you imagine the mass panic? Fear will be rampant. People having coffee in cafes will be frozen in fear as some of their friends disappear before their eyes.

Husbands will awake to find their wives gone and vice versa. It will be a time of horrifying terror. How is the disappearance of hundreds of thousands explained? Enter the Antichrist. But before we go there in our study, let's take a look at what else happens to Christians who have all gone to be with Jesus at the time of The Rapture.

The Judgement Seat of Christ

The Judgement Seat of Christ and The Great White Throne Judgement are often thought to be one and the same event. In fact, they take place at two separate times and are two different events. The Judgement Seat takes place after The Rapture when we are all with Jesus. It is for Christians. The Marriage Supper is celebrated when Jesus takes His bride; Jesus is the husband and the Church His bride. The Great White Throne Judgement takes place at the end of the Millennial reign of Christ. It is for those who have rejected Christ as Savior. We'll discuss the Great White Throne Judgement later on in our study.

We might ask at this point, where will we be when we partake of the bridal supper? When Jesus meets us in the air at The Rapture, where does He take us? To answer that question I refer to John 14:1-3: *"Don't let your heart be troubled. Trust in God, trust also in Me. There is more than enough room in my Father's home. If this were not so, would I have told you that I am going to prepare a place for you? When everything is ready, I will come and get you, so that you will always be with me where I am."* Later, after Jesus rose again and the Holy Spirit brought back to the disciples' memory the things Jesus had said to them, they would have seen this with fresh eyes. They would have understood the illustration Jesus used of the groom and the bride, and the great feast of celebration that would take place after the wedding ceremony. They would also have culturally understood that the groom always prepared rooms attached to His father's house. These rooms would be the home of him and his wife.

That is exactly how it will be when Jesus, the groom, comes for us, His bride. Jesus is now making our rooms ready as He said in John 14. As He is making our rooms ready, we also, as the bride, want to be ready, not ashamed or embarrassed at His coming.

Therefore, what is the answer to the question, where will Jesus take us when we are 'The Raptured'? To the City of God. We don't know the location of the City of God, but that is our eternal home. My father and mentor, the late Dr. Chuck Blair used to say, "The City of God is our address. The earth is our workplace." At the end of the Millennial reign, the

City of God comes down to the earth's atmosphere, but we'll look into that later on in our study.

As we now delve further into the subject of The Judgment Seat of Christ, let's begin by reading I Corinthians 9:24-27: *"Don't you realize that in a race everyone runs, but only one person gets the prize? So run to win! All athletes are disciplined in their training. They do it to win a prize that will fade away, but we do it for an eternal prize. So I run with purpose in every step. I am not just shadowboxing. I discipline my body like an athlete, training it to do what it should. Otherwise, I fear that after preaching to others I myself might be disqualified."*

I admit that for many years I had no understanding of this section of

Scripture. I completely had the wrong idea of what Paul was talking about when he wrote these words. It used to scare me because I thought he was referring to salvation and eternal security.

I was raised and taught to believe that once saved, always saved. I never believed one could lose their salvation. I am still wonderfully convinced that, just as the Scriptures teach, when we receive Jesus we are sealed for eternity. Even so, the above passage made me question. What if I am wrong? What if I work hard to be a "good" Christian but end up blowing it because of some returning sin? Will I then be "disqualified" as Paul wrote? I am delighted and relieved to share with you that our salvation is intact all for eternity! The above passage isn't speaking of salvation but of the importance of living as Christ would have us live. It's a call to live holy. The entire Bible is the written instruction and encouragement for us to walk godly and holy. That is so very important; yet what does it mean, we could be "disqualified"?

It's all to do with the Judgement Seat of Christ. There has been much misunderstanding concerning what happens at the Judgement Seat. I was one of those who was absolutely fearful about this event. In fact, I used to think to myself that the Judgement Seat will be the worst thing about heaven — as if there is a worse thing in heaven!

When I was a young Christian, I would hear older Christians talk about us having to give account of our sins. They would describe the Judgement

Seat as a place where one at a time we would be called to come forward. When we did, our lives would be played for all to see. Every sin would be revealed to everyone. It was a nightmare to even think about. Such thoughts plagued me for a long time. I did my best to push all thoughts of the Judgement Seat from my mind, such was my fear.

Wonderfully, as I grew older and the Holy Spirit led me into deeper truth, my fears faded away. Relief! We must remember what the Scriptures teach. For one thing, never forget that when we confess our sins to the Lord, He not only forgives them, but the Scriptures tell us that He no longer even remembers them. That truth is found in Hebrews 8:12: *"And I will forgive their wickedness, and I will never again remember their sins."*

Therefore, if He no longer remembers our sins, He can't play them on a larger than life screen for all to see.

I also heard it said that confessed sin would not be played back, only any unconfessed sin at the time of The Rapture. Well, that goes against the pure love of God for us. He gave His only Son to die an agonizing death to pay the penalty for our sins. Why then would He want to shame us by revealing our sins to all others waiting their own fearful turn at this terrorizing revelation of unconfessed sins? He would not gleefully rub His hands together at the moment of The Rapture to see who got caught in sin and shout, "Ah ha! Gotcha!" The pure love of God would not behave in this manner.

The truth is, the Judgement Seat of Christ has nothing at all to do with our sins. It has to do with rewards. The above passage about being "disqualified" has to do with what rewards we will not receive at the Judgement Seat. That is why Paul uses the illustration of runners in a race to win a prize. The prize isn't salvation. Paul is addressing those who are already Christians. The prize is rewards for how we have lived our lives on earth.

Paul was extremely careful how he lived his life. He desired to live holy in every aspect of his being. He wanted his words, actions, and his thoughts to be God honoring. He was encouraging us to live likewise. Why? Why be so concerned with receiving rewards? Surely being in heaven is reward enough. It's only by God's grace that we are granted entrance. So why be concerned with rewards?

For me, such a desire came when I began to delve into the book of Revelation. In Revelation 4:10 we read: *"The twenty-four elders fall down and worship the One sitting on the throne (the One who lives forever and ever) and they lay their crowns before the throne."* They cast their crowns at Jesus' feet in an act of worship. This touched me with an intense desire to make certain that I would also have something to lay at His feet in my own worship. What could you and I possibly have to give? Our rewards.

Years ago I was visiting America, traveling and speaking in various churches, sharing what God had been doing on the mission field where I was serving. During one particular visit I was invited to speak at a Vacation Bible School. I marched into the auditorium with the teachers and children to take our seats. There we pledged allegiance to the American flag, the Christians flag, and the Bible. We sang songs and listened to the announcements. Then an offering was taken before the assembly was dismissed, at which time each group of children would go to their classes with their teachers.

I happened to be sitting in the row behind my mother and her class of children. As the offering plate began to be passed along each row, a little girl sitting next to my mother looked up to her in distress. I heard the girl whisper in alarm, "I don't have anything to give." My mother smiled and discreetly reached into her pocket and produced a coin. "You can give this," she said. Sheer relief swept over the little one's face. I watched her as she kept her eyes on the offering plate. When it came down her row she proudly placed the coin on the plate, glancing at my mother again, joy dancing in her eyes.

I often think of that scene when I think about the Judgement Seat of Christ. By God's grace and mercy we will be granted into His presence. In his vast love, He will reward us for living holy so, like the little girl who came with nothing but was given a coin, we, too, will have something to give when the time of worship comes.

Imagine how you will feel if you have truly received God's gift of salvation, but then never looked into His Word to know how best to live. Choosing to obey God and live in holiness benefits us. God loves us so very much that He wants us, as pilgrims passing through our life on earth, to live with His joy and peace and guidance. Trying to conjure up our own peace is temporary at best. So, why wouldn't we want to follow Him closely, and then to top it off, be rewarded for it? Let's make certain we live in a manner so as not to be disqualified from receiving rewards. We will want something to give in worship.

Before we leave this subject, let's look at two other passages of Scripture that are often misconstrued. This will help us cement our own understanding of salvation and rewards.

The first is II Corinthians 5:1-10: *"For we know that when this earthly tent we live in is taken down (that is, when we die and leave this earthly body), we will have a house in heaven, an eternal body made for us by God Himself and not by human hands. We grow weary in our present bodies, and we long to put on our heavenly bodies like new clothing. For we will put on heavenly bodies; we will not be spirits without bodies. While we live in these earthly bodies, we groan and sigh, but it's not that we want to die and get rid of these bodies that clothe us. Rather, we want to put on our new bodies so that these dying bodies will be swallowed up by life. God Himself has prepared us for this, and as a guarantee, He has given us His Holy Spirit. So we are always confident, even though we know that as long as we live in these bodies we are not at home with the Lord. For we live by believing and not by seeing. Yes, we are fully confident, and we would rather be away from these earthly bodies, for then we will be at home with the Lord. So whether we are here in this body or away from this body, our goal is to please Him.* [1]**For we must all stand before Christ to be judged. We will each receive whatever we deserve for the good or evil we have done in this earthly body"** (emphasis added).

Paul is speaking to Christians here. He affirms that all Christians stand before Him to be judged. Remember, we are not judged for our sins (that penalty has been paid by Jesus). Nevertheless, we are judged according to our deeds which will determine our rewards - *"We will receive whatever we deserve for the good or evil we have done."* If Jesus paid for our sin, and indeed He has done so, why does Paul say we will receive what we deserve for the good or evil we have done?

To answer that question let's look at I Corinthians 3:12-15. In preceding verses of chapter 3, Paul has been affirming that Jesus Christ is our foundation. That thought in mind, he then writes beginning in verse 12, *"Anyone who builds on that foundation may use a variety of materials — gold, silver, jewels, wood, hay, or straw. But on the judgement day, fire will reveal what kind of work each builder has done. The fire will show if a person's work has any value. If the work survives, that builder will receive a reward. But if the work is burned up, the builder will suffer great loss. The builder will be saved, but like someone barely escaping through a wall of flames."*

This passage also conjures up perplexing questions. What is meant by *"the fire will show if a person's work has any value"*? Also, what is meant by *"if the work is burned up, the builder will suffer great loss"*?

To begin answering these questions we need to look again at Revelation 1:14 when John describes Jesus. *"His head and His hair were white like wool, as white as snow. And His eyes were like flames of fire."* Remember, as previously learned in Part Two, white hair and eyes denote wisdom and judgement. In Scripture, white or gray hair is referred to one who has wisdom as is mentioned in Proverbs 16:31, *"A gray head is a crown of glory; it is found in the way of righteousness."* The eyes of fire refers to nothing being hidden before God. Hebrews 4:13 reads, *"Nothing in all creation is hidden from God. Everything is naked and* **exposed before His eyes** (emphasis added)*, and He is the one to whom we are accountable."*

From the above Scriptures, we gain understanding into the passage of I Corinthians 3:12-15. You see, it is the fire of Jesus' gaze that reveals what kind of works, if any, we have done in His name. Our motives cannot be hidden. His eyes see right through us. If righteous motives are revealed beneath His penetrating gaze, then rewards are given. If unrighteousness is revealed, then rewards are like a puff of smoke. Nothing. What is the great loss we will suffer as stated in the same passage? Joy. When we stand before Him as rewards are distributed, we suddenly realize that we have absolutely nothing to give to

Him. Instead of great joy, we will sense great shame and regret.

Remember, our understanding will be complete. We will comprehend as never before, just what Jesus did for us on the cross. We will so want something to lay at His feet, but like the little girl in Vacation Bible School, fearful of the offering plate because she had nothing to give, Jesus will be giving no rewards, as my mother gave to the little girl. Our opportunity to receive something to give back to Him is today. If we refuse to delight ourselves in God, then will our salvation remain intact? Oh, yes. However, we will be saved as the passage in I Corinthians 3:12-15 declares, *"like someone barely escaping a wall of flames."* We most certainly don't want to meet Jesus having done nothing in gratitude for what He has done for us.

In conjunction with rewards, there is then The Wedding Feast. Jesus Himself gives an illustration of this fact when He points to the time of The Rapture in Matthew 25:1-13:"*Then the Kingdom of Heaven will be like ten bridesmaids who took their lamps and went to meet the bridegroom. Five of them were foolish, and five were wise. The five who were foolish didn't take enough olive oil for their lamps, but the other five were wise enough to take along extra oil. When the bridegroom was delayed, they all became drowsy and fell asleep. At midnight they were aroused by the shout, 'Look! The bridegroom is coming! Come out and meet him!' All the bridesmaids got up and prepared their lamps. Then the five foolish ones* asked the others, 'Please give us some of your oil because our lamps are going out.' But the others replied, 'We don't have enough for all of us. Go to a shop and buy some for yourselves.' But while they were gone to buy oil, the bridegroom came. **Then those who were ready went in with him to the marriage feast, and the door was locked** (emphasis added). Later, when the other five bridesmaids returned, they stood outside calling. 'Lord! Lord! Open the door for us!' But he called back, 'Believe me. I don't know you!' So you, too, must keep watch! For you do not know the day or hour of my return.'"

When Jesus gave this illustration, His listeners would have immediately understood what He was saying to them because it was a part of their culture. It has to do with the time of the engagement and the wedding ceremony. In Bible times, when a couple became engaged, they were as good as married except they did not yet live together or have sexual relations. The engagement was a binding contract and a time to make ready for life together as a married couple.

The groom had the responsibility of building a room or rooms onto his parent's home where he and his bride would live after the wedding ceremony. The bride would be at her parent's home getting ready for the time when her groom would appear. It was all done with a sense of great fun and anticipation. The bride was not forewarned when the groom would come. He could even appear in the middle of the night and call for her.

Therefore, she and her bridesmaids were busy sewing the bride's clothing, making things for the home, perhaps curtains and candles and coverings for the furniture. When the time came for her to go into her new home, she would be ready to decorate it for herself and her husband.

While the bride didn't know when the groom would appear to claim her as his own, neither did the groom know. It was the responsibility of the groom's father to oversee the building and readying of the room or rooms. Only the groom's father could announce to his son when all was in order, "Go get your bride and bring her home."

Does that remind you of something else Jesus told His followers in referring to The Rapture? In Matthew 24:36 Jesus said, *"No one knows the day or hour when these things will happen, not even the angels in heaven or the Son Himself.* **Only the Father knows"** *(emphasis added).*

When the groom came for his bride, there was a great wedding celebration with an enormous feast for all the guests. There was singing and dancing and eating for days, such was the joy of the marriage. That's how it will be at the time of The Rapture. When our groom comes to meet His bride, the Church, we will have a great celebration of rewards and a wedding feast, as the Lord's illustration of the bridesmaids indicates. Therefore, we see the order of The Rapture, The Judgement Seat where we receive rewards, and then the Wedding or Marriage Feast.

This brings us to another matter to clear up. Some theologians believe the wedding feast comes at Jesus' second coming. There is a feast at His Second Coming but it's not the marriage or wedding feast. There are, in fact, three feasts. We don't want to confuse them. I call these feasts The Wedding Feast, The Vulture's Feast, and the Kingdom Feast. We will discuss these near the end of our next section.

The Tribulation

The Tribulation is ushered in by the Rapture. Most theologians believe that the time of tribulation is seven years. Others believe it to be only half that long. I can only share what I believe to be correct from my own study, that is the number of seven years. Using your spiritual deep sea diving tools, do your own study. Look in the books of Daniel, Revelation, and Matthew.

Remember, when The Rapture takes place, the world will be in absolute chaos and terror because of the sudden disappearance of Christians. Millions of people will be gone — poof — in the blink of an eye. This is a perfect opportunity for someone to come on the scene who can give an explanation that will make sense to the world, offering some amount of calm. Enter the Antichrist. I can't even conjure a guess as to what the explanation will be. He will also design programs to restore the earth and nations to order after its mass chaos. People will be in awe of this person. They will be deceived into believing anything he says. The Antichrist is a man who is charming, handsome, and persuasive. Therefore, he has the whole world hanging onto his every word.

Before we proceed, let us define exactly what the Bible means when it refers to the time of Tribulation. You will recall that Greek word for tribulation is THLIPSIS meaning to crush or squeeze. It was used to denote crushing or grinding of pulses (edible dry peas, lentils) and grapes, and also expressed how crushing was used as torture. We discussed this in the Letter to the Church at Smyrna. Thus, the greek word for tribulation denotes a terrifying and wretched time of being crushed. It will be the worst time of terror the world has ever experienced.

Jesus had something to say concerning this horrific time on earth in Matthew 24:5-14: *"Many will come in my name claiming, 'I am the Messiah.' They will deceive many. And you will hear of wars and threats of wars, but don't panic. Yes, these things must take place, but the end won't follow immediately. Nation will go to war against nation, and kingdom against kingdom. There will be famines and earthquakes in many parts of the world. But all this is only the first of the birth pains, with more to come. Then you will be arrested, persecuted, and killed. You will be hated all over the world because you are my followers. And many will turn away from me and betray and hate each other. And many false prophets will appear and will deceive many people. Sin will be rampant everywhere, and the love of many will grow cold. But the one who endures to the end will be saved. And the Good News about the Kingdom will be preached throughout the whole world, so that all nations will hear it, and then the end will come."*

Reading this we may rightly say all of what Jesus said is happening now; however, are the present happenings actually referring to The Tribulation? It is indeed true that there have been weather disasters, wars, and persecutions of Christians in various parts of the world throughout the centuries. In fact, in the last 20 years, and even in the last year of 2020 as I write this, there has been an incredible rise in destruction by weather alone. What does this increase mean? The earth is in birth pains, as Jesus told us in Matthew 24:8 *"But all this is only the first of the birth pains with more to come."*

Our world right now is in labor, waiting to give birth to The Tribulation which will hold the most disastrous weather calamities the world has ever seen.

Do we have any details of what the weather will be like in The Tribulation? Yes. Besides what we read in Matthew 24, Revelation 6:12-14 reveals the following: *"I watched as the Lamb broke the sixth seal, and there was a great earthquake. The sun became as dark as black cloth, and the moon became as red as blood. Then the* stars of the sky fell to the earth like green figs fallen from a tree shaken by a strong wind. The sky was rolled up like a scroll, and all the mountains and islands were moved from their places."

Also in Revelation 8:7-11 we read: "The first angel blew his trumpet, and hail and fire mixed with blood were thrown down on the earth. One third of the earth was set on fire, one third of the trees were burned, and all the green grass was burned. Then the second angel blew his trumpet, and a great mountain of fire was thrown into the sea. One third of the water in the sea became blood, one third of all things living in the sea died, and one third of all the ships on the sea were destroyed. Then the third angel blew his trumpet, and a great star fell from the sky, burning like a torch. It fell on one third of the rivers *and on the springs of water. The name of the star was Bitterness. It made one third of the water bitter, and many people died from drinking the bitter water."*

Can you picture this? The strongest earthquakes ever measured will violently shake the ground in multiple places, asteroids will plummet to the earth, mountains will crumble and slip into the sea. As a result, tsunamis will surge with a vengeance. The oceans and rivers will be poisoned by these natural disasters. It's hard to imagine that anyone will survive; but they will, and they will continue to look to the Antichrist to lead them forward.

During this time of unprecedented disaster, nations will pledge their allegiance to the Antichrist as he designs survival plans. They will be deceived into believing he is the best leader the world has ever seen. The Antichrist will even make a peace treaty between Israel and all its surrounding enemies. The treaty will be drawn up for seven years but will be broken in just three and one-half years. Israel will be so deceived that they will let down their guard. They will practically dismantle their military, such will be their deluded trust in the Antichrist.

Even in the midst of this Tribulation, we see the love and mercy of God at work. What? Love and mercy when the earth and tens of thousands of people are destroyed? Yes. We see this in Matthew 24:14: *"And the Good News about the Kingdom will be preached throughout the whole world, so that all nations will hear it, and then the end will come."* Worldwide revival such as has never been seen will wonderfully take place in the midst of the world's most tumultuous times. God doesn't have to do this, but His love compels Him. Never forget *"For God so loved the world..."* The heart of God *"is not willing that any should perish,"* as we are reminded in II Peter 3:9 (KJV). How will such a revival happen in the midst of the world's greatest tragedy? Enter more players on the stage of The Tribulation: the two witnesses and the 144,000 witnesses.

The two witnesses are mentioned in Revelation 11, and the 144,000 witnesses are mentioned in Revelation 7 and 14. Let's begin with the 144,000. There has been much speculation as to who these are, but in this matter the Bible is very clear. In Revelation 7:4 we read the following:

"And I heard how many were marked with the seal of God — 144,000 were sealed from all the tribes of Israel."

The next four verses list the twelve tribes of Israel: Judah, Reuben, Gad, Asher, Naphtali, Manasseh, Simeon, Levi, Issachar, Zebulun, Joseph, and Benjamin. These verses also tell us that from each of the tribes comes 12,000 witnesses with the seal of God. 12,000 times 12 equals 144,000. While there are some gray areas in the Bible, it is very clear as to the identity of the 144,000 witnesses. Remember the promise that God gave to Abraham in Genesis 15:5: *"Then the Lord took Abram outside and said to him, 'Look up into the sky and count the stars if you can. That's how many descendants you will have.'"* Indeed, that has and will be so, even until the Millennial reign of Christ.

The question may come, "What is the seal of God that will be upon them?" This seal will protect them from death. Throughout the terrors of The Tribulation, these witnesses will be spared and unharmed. Nevertheless, I can find no hint as to what the seal will be. It reminds me of the mark that God put upon Cain after he killed his brother. That story is recorded in Genesis 4. What was the mark? Again, no hint is given.

We don't know the definition of the seal upon the 144,000, but we do know that they will be used by God to declare the Gospel of Jesus Christ, and we do know that this will spark the greatest revival the world has ever seen. Isn't that amazing news? People left behind in the time of The Rapture will have the opportunity to come to Jesus. In doing so, they will most likely be killed by instruction of the Antichrist because they will refuse the mark of the beast. We will get to that a bit later.

Let us now look at the two witnesses mentioned in Revelation 11:3: *"I will give power to my two witnesses, and they will be clothed in burlap and will prophesy during those 1,260 days."* In the preceding verse we learn that the godless of this world *"will trample the Holy City for 42 months."* The Holy City is Jerusalem. 1,260 days equals 42 months, which equals three and one-half years, which is the first half of the Tribulation. This is how long the two witnesses will be preaching on the earth.

There is speculation as to who the two witnesses are. The Bible does not reveal exactly, but our human nature cannot help but speculate. Do I have my own opinion? Yes, and I will share my thoughts; but I stress, no one knows for certain. My personal speculation comes largely from Revelation 11:5-6: *"If anyone tries to harm them, fire flashes from their mouths and consumes their enemies. This is how anyone who harms them must die. They have power to shut the sky so that no rain will fall for as long as they prophesy. And they have the power to turn the rivers and the oceans into blood, and to strike the earth with every kind of plague as often as they wish."* In the Old Testament, Elijah was given power from God to declare that it would not rain upon the earth.

This is recorded in I Kings 17:1: *"Now Elijah, who was from Tishbe in Gilead, told King Ahab, 'As surely as the Lord, the God of Israel, lives — the God I serve — there will be no dew or rain during the next few years until I give the word.'"*

In Exodus chapters 5-11 we read the story of how God led Moses to bring about the release of the Israelites from the bondage of the Egyptians. The Pharaoh refused Moses' request at first, but one plague after another finally made Pharoh relent and set the people free to follow Moses. One of the plagues mentioned in chapter 7 is the turning of water into blood. There was an array of plagues that Moses pronounced upon the land until the Israelites were finally released to him.

Also, we know that Elijah did not die but was taken to heaven in a chariot pulled by horses. There was fire all around and a great wind. The story is recorded in II Kings 2:11-12. Moses died, but you will find in Deuteronomy 34:5-6 that the Lord buried Moses and kept the place secret. Were Elijah and Moses intended for a later mission? An interesting thought.

It is for these reasons that I am making an educated guess that the two witnesses may well be Elijah and Moses. While there are some theologians who have the same thought, there are others who do not. I repeat, the Bible doesn't categorically tell us, but it's fun at times to dig into Scripture and wonder.

Try to imagine what life will be like during this time of the two witnesses. Water will be turned into blood! Neither crops nor animals will have water to sustain them, resulting in the death of masses of people and animals alike. There will be unprecedented worldwide famine. I must state again, the seven years of Tribulation will see catastrophe and tragedy, pain and death like never before in history. Understanding these things now will help us warn others of what is to come. The warnings may not be heeded. We may be laughed at and scorned for our warnings to others. So was Noah.

When Noah warned the people of the flood that would bring destruction upon the earth, he was laughed at and mocked for his warnings. Even so, he kept building the ark, gathered the animals and his family, and when it was time God Himself shut the door as we are told in Genesis 7:16: *"A male and female of each kind entered just as God had commanded Noah. Then the Lord closed the door behind them."*

When God shut the door to the ark, it was no longer possible for anyone remaining on earth to enter. Noah had given his warnings. The people knew but did not believe. They did not take heed. It will be exactly like that at the time of The Rapture. It was too late for the people in the time of Noah to be saved from the flood. It will be too late for those who refuse Jesus to be saved from The Tribulation.

Now, let's return to the two witnesses in Revelation 11:7-10: *"When they complete their testimony, the beast that comes up out of the bottomless pit will declare war against them, and he will conquer them and kill them. And their bodies will lie in the main street of Jerusalem, the city that is figuratively called 'Sodom' and 'Egypt,' the city where the Lord was crucified. And for three and a half days, all peoples, tribes, languages, and nations will stare at their bodies. No one will be allowed to bury them. All the people who belong to this world will gloat over them and give presents to each other to celebrate the death of the two prophets who tormented them."*

As we read this passage we see a horrible scene unfolding. For three and one-half years the two witnesses will boldly proclaim that Jesus is the Savior of the world. They will not candy-coat sin. They will name it and declare the only way to be forgiven and to be set free for eternity is to trust in Jesus Christ. The world's leaders will detest their message.

The two witnesses are at this time in Jerusalem. It is here that the Antichrist, also called the beast, will have the two witnesses killed. Then, because of the Antichrist's hatred for the two witnesses along with so many in the world, he will refuse their burial. In fact, he will make this a time of celebration.

Imagine the scene that unfolds: news crews will be there from around the world, cameras will show the rotting bodies of the two witnesses, people will actually exchange gifts with each other in celebration. It will be bigger than Christmas. In the world's estimation, the Antichrist will be elevated to the status of a god for his ability to rid the world of these two witnesses that plagued them with the truth.

However, as the Scripture tells us, after three and one-half days God Almighty will breathe life into them and they will stand up! Remember, the world will be watching via television and Internet This will be the most alarming breaking news ever! When the two witnesses stand up, a voice from heaven is heard to command, "Come up here!" (verse 12) Then, the Scripture tells us, they will rise into the air, disappearing into a cloud with the whole world watching.

As if that isn't enough sensation for the media, at that same moment a terrible earthquake will shake the city, killing 7000 people. The Scripture tells us that, as a result, many will give glory to God; but of course, not all. The Antichrist will be furious, his heart of evil fanned into flaming hatred.

Now let's look at the next major event that takes place, also in Jerusalem. We read this in Revelation 13:3: *"I saw that one of the heads of the beast seemed wounded beyond recovery — but the fatal wound was healed! The whole world marveled at this miracle and gave allegiance to the beast."* What happened here? Someone has assassinated the Antichrist! We don't know who, and we don't know how. What we do know is that Satan was allowed to restore life to the Antichrist.

I wonder if the resurrection of the two witnesses caused some people to question the greatness of the Antichrist. After all, he may have had the two witnesses killed, but he couldn't keep God from raising them to life. So Satan, referred to as the dragon, resurrects the Antichrist. In the minds of many, this event at the very least, equated the Antichrist to God. We see this in the next verse, 13:4: *"They worshipped the dragon for giving the beast such power, and they also worshipped the beast. 'Who is as great as the beast?' they exclaimed. 'Who is able to fight against him?'"* Do you sense the frenzy?

Now things really become horrendous. Let's read Revelation 13:5-7: "Then the beast was allowed to speak great blasphemies against God. And he was given authority to do whatever he wanted for 42 months. And he spoke terrible words of blasphemy against God, slandering His name and His dwelling — that is, those who dwell in heaven. And the beast was allowed to wage war against God's holy people and to conquer them. And he was given authority to rule over every tribe and people, and language, and nation."

The 42 months are the last three and one-half years of the Tribulation. The full fury of the beast (Antichrist) has been unleashed and he is now completely controlled by the dragon (Satan). In his war against God's holy people, meaning those who have become Christians as a result of the world's greatest revival and of the testimony of the two witnesses, we read in verse 10 of this same chapter 13: *"Anyone who is destined for prison will be taken to prison. Anyone destined to die by the sword will die by the sword. This means that God's holy people must endure persecution and remain faithful."* As I read this I am reminded again of the importance in sharing the Good News of Jesus with everyone. While it will be possible to receive salvation through Jesus during The Tribulation, it will most likely result in a sentence of prison, death, or both. It's much better to receive Jesus now and be taken out by way of The Rapture.

Upon this already horrendous scene enters another player on the stage of The Tribulation: the beast of the earth or the false prophet. John tells us in Revelation 13:11-15: *"Then I saw another beast come up out of the earth. He had two horns like those of a lamb, but he spoke with the voice of a dragon. He exercised all the authority of the first beast, whose fatal wound had been healed. He did astounding miracles, even making fire flash down to earth from the sky while everyone was watching. And with all the miracles he was allowed to perform on behalf of the first beast, he deceived all the people who belong to this world. He ordered the people to make a great statue of the first beast, who was fatally wounded and then came back to life. He was then permitted to give life to this statue so that it could speak. Then the statue of the beast commanded that anyone refusing to worship it must die."*

This is a very telling portion of scripture. We see how the second beast, also known as the false prophet, will deceive people because of the miracles he performs.

Do you remember the story of Moses when he was sent by God to the Pharaoh of Egypt? God commanded Moses to demand the Israelites be set free. Moses was given power from God to perform miracles, but surprisingly,

Pharaoh's court sorcerers also had power. In the story recorded in Exodus 7:8-12, Moses tells his brother, Aaron, to throw down his staff. Aaron did, and the staff turned into a snake. Pharaoh's magicians did the same thing. However, the snake from Aaron's staff swallowed up the snakes of the magicians. Even so, Pharaoh's heart remained hardened to the truth of God.

This is how it will be during this time of Tribulation. Because of the Internet and social media, people from every nation will watch live the resurrection of the two witnesses who had been dead in the street. Even so, because the Antichrist had been assassinated and rose to life, people's already hardened hearts will remain blind to the saving truth of Jesus Christ. Therefore, when the false prophet arrives on the scene performing miracles, they will be deceived by his power, either not understanding or not caring that the power is satanic. In this satanic power, the next miracle will be that of the talking statue.

I can remember many years ago visiting Disney World in Orlando, Florida. One of my favorite attractions was the Country Bears. Mechanical, lifelike bears would talk and sing. We all knew they weren't real, of course, but the pretense was great fun.

When the statue of the Antichrist is built and given life so that it can talk, it won't be pretense and it won't be fun. People will be terror-stricken! They will know there is nothing mechanical or digital in the talking statue. They will know that it has miraculously received life.

The statue will utter words that will fill everyone with fear and dread. It has already declared that anyone who did not worship it would be put to death. Let's read further in Revelation 13:16-17: "He required everyone — small and great, rich and poor, free and slave — to be given a mark on the right hand or on the forehead. And no one could buy or sell anything without that mark, which was either the name of the beast or the number representing his name."

I've often heard Christians say that they are fearful of accidentally receiving the mark of the beast. Let me assure you that this will not be possible for two reasons. First, any Christians reading this now, before The Rapture has taken place, will not even be on earth when the mark of the beast is given. Second, those who have become Christians during this time of Tribulation will fully understand what taking the mark means, and they will refuse. It will be totally clear that this mark is a sign of worship and allegiance to the Antichrist.

I've heard people speculate and reason that Christians, of course, would not take the mark, but they could just hide away and ride it out until Jesus returns to set up his Millennial Reign. A reasonable thought but not possible. Read verse 17 again. It plainly tells us that without the mark, no one can buy or sell anything at all. Also, no kind neighbor or friend can buy or sell for you. It would be certain death if they were discovered doing such a thing.

Christians will refuse the mark of the beast; in doing so, they will either be killed or they will die of starvation. However, for those who take the mark, life as they have known it will be over. Let's look further into this by reading Revelation 14:9-11: *"Then a third angel followed them, shouting, 'Anyone who worships the beast and his statue or who accepts the mark on the forehead or on the hand must drink the wine of God's anger. It has been poured full strength into God's cup of wrath. And they will be tormented with fire and burning sulfur in the presence of the holy angels and the Lamb. The smoke of their torment will rise forever and ever, and they will have no relief day or night, for they have worshipped the beast and his statue, and have accepted the mark of his name.'"*

Do you see how accepting the mark of the beast is not something that will be done by accident? The choice will be clear.

For those who have received Jesus during this Tribulation time, let's read further in Revelation 14:12-13: "This means that God's holy people must endure persecution patiently, obeying His commands and maintaining their faith in Jesus. And I heard a voice from heaven saying, 'Write this down: Blessed are those who die in the Lord from now on. Yes, says the Spirit, they are blessed indeed, for they will rest from their hard work; for their good deeds follow them!'"

These seven years of Tribulation will be the most dark, evil time in all of history. Do you see why it's so very important that we urge our family, friends, neighbors, and colleagues to please receive Jesus' gift of salvation now so they may escape this time of dreadful evil? Time is short. Signs point that the end is near.

Are there particular signs that point to the nearness of The Rapture? No. Are there signs that point to the nearness of The Tribulation? Yes. That's important to us because when we know the Tribulation is near, we know The Rapture comes first!

There are three particular signs that keep me listening for the trumpet which sounds the arrival of Jesus in the air at the time of The Rapture. Let's take a look at them:

1. The Nation of Israel. Israel astonished the world when, in 1948, it became a nation in its own right. Why is this an important sign? Because the

Antichrist makes a peace treaty between Israel and all her surrounding enemies. The treaty will be for seven years, but it will be broken in three and one-half years. There could be no peace treaty in the time of Tribulation without Israel being a nation. Therefore, since 1948, this event has excited the Christian community with the nearness of Christ's return by The Rapture.

2. Evil in the world. Let's look again at Matthew 24. Verses 36-44 deal with The Rapture. The preceding verses deal with The Tribulation. We are going to read 37-39 which points to the evil of the world at this time, *"When the Son of Man returns, it will be* **like it was in Noah's day** *(emphasis added).* In those

days before the flood, the people were enjoying banquets and parties and weddings right up to the time Noah entered his boat. People didn't realize what was going to happen until the flood came and swept them all away. That is the way it will be when the Son of Man comes."

Doesn't that describe the shape of our world today? Nations are doing things that at one time was unimaginable. I was a child in the '60's. Going to church was seen as respectable. Christians and non-Christians alike saw marriage as God intended — between one man and one woman, and it was commonly believed that life begins at conception. Prayer was honored in public places and considered an act of decency. I would have never dreamed that in my life time homosexuality, transgender lifestyle, and the mass killing of unborn children would not only be accepted but applauded. I never dreamed that public prayer would be seen as despicable. I never dreamed that Christians in western nations would be threatened with prosecution for "hate crimes" for standing up for God's principles. (Pastors in Australia, the UK, and the USA have had to appear in court for refusing to marry gay couples. Thus far the cases have been dismissed and no jail time served. However, the fact that the arrests were ever made is astonishing.) What has happened? **The world has become as it was in the days of Noah.**

3. Weather disasters, disease, false messiahs, and wars among the nations. Matthew 24:4-8: *"Jesus told them, 'Don't let anyone mislead you, for many will come in my name, claiming, 'I am the messiah.' They will deceive many. And you will hear of wars and threats of wars, but don't panic. Yes, these things must take place but the end won't follow immediately. Nation will go to war against nation, and kingdom against kingdom. There will be famines and earthquakes in many parts of the world. But all this is only the first of the*

birth pains with more to come.'" I am writing this book in early 2021. As I reflect upon 2020, it has been an incredible year of signs of the end times as mentioned in the passage above. I list several which have been record-breaking:

4. Australian bushfires damaged 186 million hectares and killed countless animals, especially among its native koala bears and kangaroos.

5. Jakarta, Indonesia was devastated by floods. Water rose five feet throughout the city, causing landslides and many deaths by electrocution from live wires in the water.

6. The Philippines saw its worst volcanic eruption in 43 years which caused over 2000 earthquakes in the area.

7. Jamaica, Turkey, and Russia experienced 45 earthquakes registering at least 6 on the Richter scale.

8. East Africa, India, and Pakistan have been hit by unprecedented swarms of locusts, the worst in 30 years, devastating crops.

9. India and Bangladesh have suffered tremendous damage and loss of life from Cyclone Amphan.

10. Across Europe, windstorms Cione and Alex caused 66 billion dollars

in damages.

11. South Korea experienced monsoon rains and landslides.

12. Storm Gloria hit Spain causing wide coastal damage.

13. Lightning strikes did significant damage in Congo, Africa.

14. A gas explosion rocked Syria.

15. Derecho winds caused destruction in Iowa, USA.

16. Tornadoes ripped through Mississippi and other southern states in the USA.

17. Hurricanes Laura, Cristobal, Marco, Delta, and Zeta did exceptional damage in Louisiana,

USA.

18. The United States was hit by 11 hurricanes in total.

19. Multiple earthquakes struck Nepal.

20. Floods and landslides were also recorded in Brazil, Cambodia, Egypt, Rwanda, and Madagascar.

21. Yellow Fever was found in Guiana and France.

22. Plague and Ebola spread through the Congo.

23. Covid 19 caused a worldwide pandemic.

Added to the above, nations around the world are facing untold civil unrest. Islamic nations desire to "wipe Israel off the map" (their words); North Korea is experimenting with long range missiles; China has gained control over much of the world's power grids; the United States, China, and Russia own nuclear weapons and these type weapons are suspected to be in Iran, Iraq, and Syria, poised and ready for attack or counter attack. In short, the whole world is a ticking time-bomb.

Continuing discussion about the mark of the beast, let's take a look at Revelation 13:18: *Wisdom is needed here. Let the one with understanding solve the meaning of the number of the beast, for it is the number of a man. His number is 666."* This is a dreadful number just because we know it represents Satan. It seems the whole world has heard about this number. Books have been written and films made. While many throughout history have speculated on the meaning of the number, there is agreement that it's an evil number representing Satan.

Dr. David Jeremiah has an interesting thought concerning the mark of the beast. He reminds us that we know the number seven is a number representing completion. There are many Biblical examples, but just look at one - the creation of the world. It was created in six days, and on the seventh day God rested from His work. It was complete. The number of man is six. Man only becomes complete when we accept Jesus Christ, which ushers in the Holy Spirit to take up residence in our lives, sealing us until the day of redemption.

Receiving God's gift of salvation through Jesus is the only way we become complete. Dr. Jeremiah wonders if the mark is as simple in meaning as the 'incompletion' of man. He stresses it's just a theory. None of us knows, but it's interesting to wonder.

In our study thus far, we see the dragon, which is Satan. We see the first beast which is the Antichrist, and we see the second beast which is the false prophet. Is there some significance in these three? Oh, yes.

Remember, Satan is an imitator of truth. He is the father of lies. In His attempts to deceive, he will counterfeit the truth in order to fool us. He has attempted something here that is tragic to those who believe it. I call it the unholy trinity.

We know that God is three in one: God the Father, God the Son, and God the Holy Spirit. God sent His Son to offer salvation to the whole world. After Jesus rose from the dead and ascended to heaven, the Holy Spirit came to inhabit those who are born again into the family of God. Keep in mind that the Holy Spirit always points to the Son.

Now, let's look at the unholy trinity: Satan sends the Antichrist. The Antichrist demands to be worshipped as if he is a god. The false prophet always points to the Antichrist. Do you see the evil deception? All those who believe in this unholy trinity during The Tribulation will suffer tragic consequences for eternity and as we read in Revelation 14:10-11, such people will suffer fire and burning sulphur, having no relief day or night. Satan whispers his lies, indeed, causing tragic deception.

As we now look at the last three and one-half years of The Tribulation, I draw your attention to Revelation 16. There is described in this chapter the seven bowls of seven plagues. I list them as follows:

1. Malignant sores break out on everyone who had the mark of the beast and who worshipped his statue - v.2.

2. The sea turns into blood and everything in the sea dies - v.3.

3. All rivers and springs turn into blood leaving no drinking water - v.4.

4. The sun burns with blasts of fire, burning everyone exposed - vs. 8-9.

5. The earth is plunged into darkness - v.10.

6. The great river Euphrates dries up, which allows enemies of Israel to march over it; attack/ demons appearing as frogs leap from the mouths of Satan, the Antichrist, and the false prophet, working miracles as they gather armies to march against Israel in what is called the Battle of Armageddon - vs.12-14 and 16.

7. The world's worst earthquake shakes the earth, causing every island to disappear, and every mountain to fall flat; a horrible storm strikes with hailstones weighing seventy-five pounds - vs.18-21.

I want to say something further concerning point 6 when the Euphrates River dries up, allowing troops from the east to march toward Israel. Did you know that it is already possible to dry up the Euphrates River? In 1990, the Ataturk Dam was completed. It's the largest of 22 dams along the Tigris and Euphrates rivers. It is located on the southern border of Turkey. Can you imagine the ease with which the enemy troops begin their march into Israel? Russia, who will lead the march, only has to contact

Turkey, make the request, and presto! The land becomes dry. This is yet another point of interest to make note of concerning today's readiness for The Tribulation to take place.

In mentioning the enemies who will march against Israel, do we know the identity of these enemies? We do. First, let's read from the prophecy written in Ezekiel 38:1-2, 5-6 and 11 (King James Version): *"This is another message that came to me from the Lord: 'Son of Man, turn and face Gog of the land of Magog, the prince who rules over the nations of Meshech and Tubal, and prophesy against him....Persia, Ethiopia, and Libya, will join you, too, with all their weapons. Gomer and all its armies will also join you, along with the armies of Beth-togarmah, from the distant north, and many others...You will say, 'Israel is an unprotected land filled with unwalled villages! I will march against her and destroy these people who live in such confidence."*

I encourage you to also read Daniel Chapter 11 which tells of the coming of the King of the North - another name for Gog.

Specifically, the countries, cities, and people involved in marching against Israel in the Battle of Armageddon are:

King of the north - Russia
Gog - Prince of Rosh (Russia)
Magog - the surrounding countries (very likely those countries that were once part of the USSR)
Meshech - Moscow
Tubal - Tobolsk (Siberia, Russia)

**Meshech and Tobolsk are inhabited by the descendants of Noah

Beth Tagarmah - Asia Minor and Turkey

Gomer - Caucuses and southern Russia

King of the East - China

Persia - Iran

King of The South - Arab/African coalition

Cush - Ethiopia

Put and Libya - North Africa

There are references to the above players on Armageddon's stage in the following passages: Ezekiel 38:1-6: *"This is another message that came to me from the Lord: 'Son of Man, turn and face Gog of the land of Magog, the prince who rules over the nations of Meshech and Tubal, and prophesy against him. Give him this message from the Sovereign Lord: Gog, I am* your enemy! I will turn around and put hooks in your jaws to lead you out with your whole army — your horses and chariots in full armor and a great horde armed with shields and swords. Persia, Ethiopia, and Libya will join you, too, with all their weapons. Gomer and all its armies will also join you, along with the armies of Beth-togarmah from the distant north, and many others.'"

Daniel 11:40-45: "Then at the time of the end, the king of the south will attack the king of the north. The king of the north will storm out with chariots, charioteers, and a vast navy. He will evade various lands and sweep through them like a flood. He will enter the glorious land of Israel, and many nations will fall, but Moab, Edom, and the best part of Ammon will escape. He will conquer many *countries, and even Egypt will not escape. He will gain control over the gold, silver, and treasures of Egypt, and tiger Libyas and Ethiopians will be his servants. But then news from the east and the north will alarm him, and he will set out in great anger to destroy and obliterate many. He will stop between the glorious holy mountain and the sea and will pitch his royal tents. But while he is there his time will suddenly run out, and no one will help him."*

Note: Moab, Edom, and Ammon are all part of Jordan today.

From these passages we see that the king of the south will attack the king of the north. This may come as a surprise because when we think of the battle at Armageddon, we picture all nations united against Israel. Keep in mind that this is a time of great, unprecedented evil in the world. Nations will collectively hate Israel, but they will also harbor hatred for each other. Each leader will be jealous of the other, desiring that they be known as the ultimate conqueror of their shared enemy Israel. While they attack each other, in the end, they concentrate their best efforts on crushing Israel.

NOTE: There is an interesting observation to make concerning Gomer and his descendants. Gomer is also a grandson of Noah. Noah's grandchildren settled all over what today is known as Russia. Keeping that in mind, I was initially confused in my study of End Times concerning who would be marching against Israel. As I read other theologians, it seemed a popular consensus that

Germany would be included. Why Germany? We have Russia and surrounding countries, and then way over in the west we have Germany marching also? I thought this strange.

This is another example of using what I call your spiritual deep sea diving tools. I began researching Bible history and came upon an exciting discovery. It was a treasure of truth that I could bring to the surface of my understanding.

During World War II in Germany, when Jews were being rounded up and taken to concentration camps, they were often referred to as the Ashkenazi. I thought this most interesting. Why were they called Ashkenazi? Diving deeper I discovered that one of Gomer's sons was named Ashkenaz. It is believed that, unlike his siblings and cousins who spread throughout Russia and surrounding countries, Ashkenaz went further west, settling in what is known today as Germany. Hence, as the descendants of Noah form an alliance to march against Israel, Germany will join with them.

Let us now discuss Armageddon. This is another word that has captured the interest and imagination of people throughout the ages. Books are written and movies made, rendering their own fictitious accounts. Such interest is especially noteworthy because the word is only mentioned once in the whole Bible. It is found in Revelation 16:16: *"And the demonic spirits gathered all the rulers and their armies to a place with the Hebrew name Armageddon."*

What does the name mean? In Hebrew the word HOR means mount while the word MEGIDDO means slaughter. There is to this day a Mount Meggido in Israel. It stands above a great plain called the Valley of Armageddon, or the valley of slaughter. It's a plain about 25 miles by 32 miles. It includes the Jezreel Valley and Mount Tabor, the lower Galilee to Tiberias and all of Nazareth. Over the centuries, the greatest generals have declared this valley to be a perfect place for battle.

It's understandable to believe the Battle of Armageddon to be one great battle. It is, in fact, many battles that take place over the last three and one-half years of the Tribulation. I compare it to World War II. WWII wasn't one long battle; it was many that took place over several years throughout Europe and Asia.

The Battle of Armageddon will be the bloodiest battle ever to take place. We learn in Revelation 14:20 that one result of this battle is as follows: *"blood flowed from the winepress in a stream about 180 miles long and as high as a horse's bridle."* Can you imagine such a horrendous sight? This horrific battle comes to an end when the King of kings and Lord of lords arrives on the scene. The Antichrist will be sitting on the throne of the temple in Jerusalem, desecrating it by proclaiming himself as God. The living statue will be commanding death to all who refuse the mark of the beast. The unholy trinity of the dragon, the Antichrist, and the false prophet will be captured, their reign of terror brought to an end. We read this in

Revelation 19:19-20: *"Then I saw the beast and the kings of the world and their armies gathered together to fight against the One sitting on the horse and His army. And the beast was captured and with him the false prophet who did mighty miracles on behalf of the beast — miracles that deceived all who had accepted the mark of the beast and who worshipped his statue. Both the beast and his false prophet were thrown alive into the fiery lake of burning sulfur."*

It is here that we now see the second banquet, the Feast of The Vultures. It takes place after the Battle of Armageddon. This battle will result in tremendous death and unprecedented bloodshed. Revelation 14:20 tells us that *"blood flowed in a stream about 180 miles long and as high as a horse's bridle."* As a result of this we read in Revelation 19:17-18, *"Then I saw an angel standing in the sun,* ***shouting to the vultures flying high in the sky: 'Come! Gather together for the great banquet God has prepared*** (emphasis added). *Come and eat the flesh of kings, generals, and strong warriors; of horses and their riders; and of all humanity, both free and slave, small and great.'"*

The Vulture's Feast comes, as we read in Revelation 19:21, in conjunction with the beast and false prophet being thrown alive into the fiery lake of burning sulfur. *"Their entire army was killed by the sharp sword that came from the mouth of the One riding the white horse.* ***And the vultures all gorged themselves on dead bodies"*** (emphasis added). This incident is also recorded in Ezekiel 39:17-24.

The third banquet, The Kingdom Feast, is mentioned in Luke 13:28-30, Luke 22:28-30, Isaiah 24:23 and Isaiah 25:6. Let's take a look at the passage in Luke 22:28-30, when Jesus says to His followers, *"You have stayed with me in my time of trial. And just as my Father has granted me a Kingdom, I now grant you the right to eat and drink at my table in my Kingdom. And you will sit on thrones, judging the twelve tribes of Israel."* This is clearly a reference to a feast that will take place in the kingdom that Jesus will set up, the Millennial Kingdom. How do we know? Because it is only during the Millennial Reign that Christians are given positions of authority to rule over others during this time. More about that later.

Let's look at one other Scripture reference, Isaiah 25:6-8: "In Jerusalem, the Lord of Heaven's Armies will spread a wonderful feast for all the people of the world. It will be a delicious banquet with clear, **well-aged wine and choice meat** (emphasis added). There He will remove the cloud of gloom, the shadow of death that hangs over the earth. He will swallow up death forever! The Sovereign Lord will wipe away all tears. He will remove forever all insults and mockery against His land and people. The Lord has spoken!" Scripture passages as these lead me to believe there will be a Kingdom Feast at the beginning of the Millennial reign of Christ.

We are told that at this banquet there will be *"well-aged wine and choice meat."* This grabbed my attention because at this time there will be no more death among God's children. Therefore, how could an animal be killed for food?

Doing some spiritual deep-sea diving I was reminded of Matthew 26:26-29. Jesus Himself is serving what we call The Lord's Supper or Communion. Jesus said they were drinking His blood and eating His body. Of course, they were not. They were drinking wine and eating bread. It was symbolic. It seems to me that the "choice meats" are also symbolic of something most tasty indeed.

Isn't all this a terrifying account of what is to come during the time of The Tribulation? Aren't you glad that as Christians we won't be a part of that dreadful time to come? Once again, I remind us all to be quick to share the

Good News of Jesus Christ with our loved ones, neighbors, and co-workers. The world's stage is set for The Tribulation to begin, and we know The Rapture comes first. The time is near.

The Millennium

The Millennial Reign of Christ lasts for one thousand years. It starts immediately at the end of The Tribulation when Christ takes His rightful place sitting on the throne of David in Jerusalem. Before we investigate the Millennium, I want to share something particularly interesting.

You will recall that the number six in the Bible is the number of man or the number of incompletion. The number seven is the perfect number of God and is the number of completion. Keeping that thought in mind, let's look at the years that have passed on earth since Adam and Eve.

When we read the book of Genesis, we discover that the period of time from

Adam to Abraham is about 2000 years. From Abraham to Jesus being born of a virgin is another 2000 years. From Jesus to the present day is approximately 2000 years. That's a total of 6000 years since Adam. The number of incompletion. Add on the Millennium and we have another 1000 years making a total of 7000 years, the number of completion. By the end of the Millennium, the number of God's children will be complete. Is that time frame another hint to us that The Rapture is imminent? I find these musings most exciting.

What do we know about the Millennium? To begin, let's read Isaiah 65:20-25: *"No longer will babies die when only a few days old. No longer will adults die before they live a full life. No longer will people be considered old at one hundred! Only* the cursed will die that young. In those days people will live in the houses they build and eat the fruit of their own vineyards. Unlike the past, invaders will not take their houses and confiscate their vineyards. For my people will live as long as trees, and my chosen ones will have time to enjoy their hard-won gains. They will not work in vain, and their children will not be doomed to misfortune. For they are people blessed by the Lord, and their children, too, will be blessed. I will answer them before they even call to me. While they are still talking about their needs, I will go ahead and answer their prayers! The wolf and the lamb will feed together. The lion will eat hay like a cow. But the snakes will eat dust. In those days no one will be hurt or destroyed on My holy mountain. I, the Lord, have spoken!"

Doesn't that sound idyllic? It will be! It will be a time of unprecedented peace and joy. Before we look more closely into the above Scripture, we must understand that during the Millennial reign there will still be those people who are what I will refer to as the 'regular' humans. You and I who are Christians at the time of The Rapture will be caught up in the air. Does it surprise you to learn that during the Millennial reign of Christ regular people will be born, will sin, and will die? It surprised me when I first came upon this fact because I was confusing the new heavens and new earth with the Millennium. Perhaps you have done the same thing.

By way of further explanation, keep in mind that the Battle of Armageddon will be the fierce and bloody battle that ushers in Christ, ending The Tribulation, and bringing in the Millennium. All this takes place in Israel, but what about the rest of the world?

There are many other countries not directly involved in this Battle of Armageddon who will have survivors. Thousands upon thousands will be killed by the horrible weather disasters and plagues, but amazingly, some survive.

Therefore, during the Millennium, there are regular humans still living, marrying, having children, and dying. This cycle of regular humans having children will last throughout the thousand years. At some point toward the end of the Millennium, the last regular human will have lived and died.

All these regular humans will have the same opportunity as you and I had - to receive Jesus or reject Him. There will be such peace that it's hard to imagine some people will reject Him, but they will. When a regular human receives Christ as Savior, they are immediately transformed at death, gaining a body that will never die. There will be no period of time in the grave. On the other hand, those regular humans who die without having received Jesus as Savior will be gone from our sight, their bodies in the grave, their souls and spirits awaiting the Great White Throne Judgment.

Jesus will be ruling on His throne in Jerusalem. I see Him as something like the Chief Justice of the Supreme Court. Around the world, Christians who have been raptured and been faithful to Him on earth will be given positions of responsibility. Revelation 2:26-27a tells us, *"To all who are victorious, who obey me to the very end, to them I will give authority over all the nations."* Therefore, we know that some of us will be given positions of judges around the world to oversee smaller matters. Because we will be without sin, we will judge fairly and without mistake.

One other group of people needs mentioning here. We read about them in Revelation 20:4: *"Then I saw thrones, and the people sitting on them had been given the authority to judge. And I saw the souls of them who had been beheaded for their testimony about Jesus and for proclaiming the Word of God. They had not worshipped the beast or his statue, nor accepted his mark on their foreheads or their hands. They all came to life again and reigned with Christ for a thousand years."* We know that nothing is in God's Word by happenstance. Everything written is inspired by the Holy Spirit, is true, and with reason.

Forty years ago I began my career as a missionary. My travels and places of service have been among persecuted Christians. For many years the ministry has been among those living in communist countries, but for the last decade plus, it has been in a growing Islamic country. Therefore, I have learned much about Muslim beliefs and practices.

In light of Revelation 20:4, I find it interesting to note that Muslims prefer beheading as their chosen method of execution. This verse categorically tells us that Christians refusing the mark of the beast will be executed by beheading. Islam is the second fastest growing religion in the world today. Is this fact, also, another hint that the time of The Rapture is near? I cannot say it enough - we must each one take every opportunity to share the saving grace of Jesus that we may all escape The Tribulation.

This verse gives assurance that all those who accept Jesus during The Tribulation will also reign with Christ for the whole of the Millennial Reign. Like you and I at the time of The Rapture, those saved during The Tribulation and The Millennium will be instantly transformed, living in perfection and ruling in positions of authority.

What other positions will the transformed Christians oversee? This will be an unprecedented time of fairness throughout the earth. Transformed Christians will be in charge of the education system; they will be professors and teachers. Transformed Christians will oversee construction and architectural projects. Transformed Christians will oversee the Arts and Theater. Transformed Christians will run the hospitals to care for those regular Christians who will still be subject to illness and accident. Transformed Christians will oversee agriculture. Every business will be overseen by transformed Christians.

It's interesting to note that there will be no bloodshed. We know this from the passage in Isaiah 65 that tells us the wolf will lie with the lamb and will eat hay like the cow. People will be vegetarians, and although transformed Christians will not need to eat in order to live, we will be allowed to enjoy eating. I'm personally glad to know I can still enjoy my favorite food of spaghetti and garlic bread, which reminds me of something else.

In our transformed bodies, we don't need cars or airplanes to travel. We will go from one place to another by mere thought. Jesus did this after he rose from the dead. We read in John 20:19 *"That Sunday evening the disciples were meeting behind closed doors because they were afraid of the Jewish leaders. Suddenly, Jesus was standing there among them! 'Peace be with you,' he said."* When we have our own transformed bodies, we will live and move from place to place by mere thought. Won't that be exciting? So,

I may simply think that I want to be in Italy for a lunch of spaghetti, and presto! I will be there. What fun we are all going to have in our transformed bodies!

What other aspects of life do we know about during the Millennial Reign of Christ? Let's go back to our passage in Isaiah 65 and reread verse 20: *"No longer will babies die when only a few days old. No longer will adults die before they have lived a full life. No longer will people be considered old at one hundred! Only the cursed will die that young."* Why is it that babies will not die? Remember, transformed Christians will be ruling and will be the doctors and nurses caring for those still in regular human bodies like we have today. Transformed Christians will have perfect knowledge. There will be medical procedures to heal and preserve life such as we have not seen. It will be beyond all the medical discoveries thus far.

Why will it be normal for adults to live beyond one hundred? In answering this question, besides advanced medical care, there is the environment to consider. Keep in mind that transformed Christians won't need cars or airplanes. That reduces carbon emissions. However, what new inventions might there be anyway that will restore our environment? It will be a most creative time on earth with transformed Christians in charge of the process.

I want to also point out that many scientists who are Christians believe that the earth's atmosphere may revert back to how it was before the flood in Genesis. Before the flood people lived for hundreds of years. It's believed that a canopy surrounded the earth keeping out the sun's dangerous UV rays. The torrential rains that brought the flood weakened that protective canopy. Remember, until the flood it had never rained upon the earth. It's thought that during the Millennium the former canopy will be restored. Our theological scientists, as I call them, readily say this is only theory, but it certainly makes sense of the longer life span during the Millennium.

Now let's explain the last phrase of Isaiah 65:20: *"Only the cursed will die that young."* Who is cursed? Keep in mind that sin is still on the earth. The regular humans still have free will to choose Jesus or not and are still subject to sin. Will there still be murders and drug abuse and sexual immorality? It will be greatly lessened because of such peace and joy throughout the earth, but yes, such sins will still take place. The cursed are those who reject Christ and become so embroiled in such sin that they could die young.

There was a time in my younger years that I did not understand how the transformed Christians could live among the regular humans who still sinned and not sin themselves. I remember saying to my father, "Dad, I bet I'll be the first one to sin during the thousand years. I'll have some bad thought and be doomed!" I was frightened at the possibility, but my Dad and mentor gave me a comforting explanation. He reminded me that Adam and Eve, and each person born since, have all been given free choice — God's way or their own way. We know the tragic consequences of Adam and Eve's choice - sin came into the world. (By the way, knowing the perfection that Adam and Eve lived in, walking and talking with God each day, and yet sinning, helps us to understand how the regular humans during the Millennial reign can also sin even in the midst of such peace and joy.) However, since Jesus redeemed us from the curse of sin, you and I, upon exercising our free will and choosing Jesus, are **sealed** as it tells us in Ephesians 1:13-14: *"...And when you believed in Christ, He identified you as His own by giving you the Holy Spirit, whom He promised long ago. The Spirit is God's **guarantee*** (emphasis added) *that He will give us the inheritance He promised..."* Jesus also tells us in His own words in John 10:28, *"I give them eternal life and they will never perish. No one can* snatch them away from me." Therefore, based on Jesus' own guarantee, we need not fear that we will sin during the Millennium.

Let us now read again Isaiah 65:21-25:   *"No longer will babies die when only a few days old.   No longer will adults die before they live a full life. No longer will people be considered old at one hundred!   Only the cursed will die that young. In those days people will live in the houses they build and eat the fruit of their own vineyards.   Unlike the past, invaders will not take their houses and confiscate their vineyards. For my people will live as long as trees, and my chosen ones will have time to enjoy their hard-won gains.   They will not work in vain, and their children will not be doomed to misfortune.   For they are people blessed by the Lord, and their children, too, will be blessed. I will answer them before they even call to me. While they are still talking about their needs, I will go ahead and answer their prayers! The wolf and the lamb will feed together. The lion will eat hay like a cow. But the snakes will eat dust. In those days no one will be hurt or destroyed on My holy mountain. I, the Lord, have spoken!"*

Imagine, the land will be blessed so that crops will grow, always yielding grain and fruit. Robbers will be almost non-existent. Should such a crime take place, justice will be swift. It won't be like it is today when cases can be held for months or even years. Jesus will have revolutionized the justice system. Therefore, such sins will be rare. I remember stories from people the age of my grandparents who talked about leaving the doors to their homes and cars unlocked when they were young. We wouldn't think of doing such a foolish thing today, but during the Millennium we will experience such trust and safety again.

The above passage in Isaiah also assures us that those who become Christians during the Millennium will not work in vain or suffer any misfortune, and Jesus promises to answer their prayers, taking care of their needs, even before they have time to ask Him! They will live without harm. Even animals will live peacefully together.

Once again I ask, can you imagine such a time of peace, joy, and safety? It will be a wonderful world during those thousand years, and it gets even better during the time of the new heavens and new earth — but first comes the time when Satan will be let loose.

I find it incredible to believe that after a thousand years of unprecedented peace on earth, that any nation could be deceived into believing they could possibly defeat Jesus who is on His throne in Jerusalem. Why would they even want to, given the splendor the world will be in at that time? Even so, that is exactly what is going to happen. We know this because it is recorded in Revelation 20:7-9: *"When the thousand years come to an end, Satan will be let out of his prison. He will go out to deceive the nations — called Gog and Magog — in every corner of the earth. He will gather them together for battle — a mighty army, as numberless as sand along the seashore. And I saw them as they went up on the broad plain of the earth and surrounded God's people and the beloved city. But fire from heaven came down on the attacking armies and consumed them."*

Satan is more awful than words can adequately describe. He lies and he deceives — not some of the time, but all of the time! You and I must always beware of his subtle deception. One of my favorite verses concerning this matter is found in Proverbs 4:23: *"Guard your heart above all else, for it determines the course of your life."* If we leave our hearts unguarded against Satan's attacks, he will send demonic influences as we discussed in Part One, and he will zap our joy and peace, rendering us ineffective. Never forget that Satan's ultimate purpose for us is to steal our peace, kill our joy, and destroy all hope. It is crucial that we remain in guard position at all times. If we do not, if we succumb to the tragic deceptions of the enemy, the consequences will be dire.

How do we keep our holy resolve intact? We have three excellent passages of instruction:

1. Philippians 4:6-7: *"Don't worry about anything; instead, pray about everything. Tell God what you need, and thank Him for all He has done. Then you will experience God's peace, which exceeds anything we can understand. His peace will guard your hearts and minds as you live in Christ Jesus."*

2. II Timothy 2:15-16: *"Work hard so you can present yourself to*

God and receive His approval. Be a good worker, one who does not need to be ashamed and who correctly explains the Word of truth. Avoid worthless, foolish talk that only leads to more godless behavior."

3. James 1:19: *"Understand this my dear brothers and sisters, you must all be quick to listen, slow to speak, and slow to get angry."*

These passages contain instructions that are vital to healthy spiritual life. Here are essential points to master:

1. **Pray** - talk to God about everything and then listen to

what the Holy Spirit says to you.

2. **Praise** - develop an attitude of thanking Him even in difficult times, growing a trust that reminds you God knows what He is allowing in your life to mold you into His image.

3. **Work hard** - have a constant goal of **praying and praising and studying His Word everyday.** Don't stop! Like an athlete building physical stamina, this will build your spiritual stamina.

4. **Beware your tongue** - senseless argument is a waste of your time. Listen well, then carefully choose your words. As the saying goes, "Better to remain silent and be thought a

fool, than to speak and remove all doubt."

Getting back to our passage in Revelation 20, notice verse 9b: "...But fire from heaven came down on the attacking armies and consumed them." Unlike the drawn out battle of Armageddon, this last attempt to overthrow God is over in an instant. If not so serious, it would be rather comical. Here are Satan's armies of Gog and Magog coming in all their might! Then — *Zap! Pssst!* Fire from heaven — it's over.

At that moment, Satan's end comes for eternity. *"Then the devil who had deceived them, was thrown into the fiery lake of burning sulphur, joining the beast and the false prophet. There they will be tormented day and night forever and ever"* (Revelation 20:10)

The Great White Throne Judgement

Next comes an event in which Christians, thankfully, will have no part. Jesus, the perfect judge who sees all and knows our intentions and every motive of our hearts, will call to account every person who has rejected Him. This is the final judgement. It is first mentioned by Jesus in John 5:28-29: *"...Indeed, the time is coming when all the dead in the graves will hear the voice of God's Son, and they will rise again. Those who have done good will rise to experience eternal life, and those who have done evil will rise to experience judgement."* Jesus began at the onset of His earthly ministry to instruct His followers on what was to come.

Then we read in Revelation 20:11-15: *"And I saw a great white throne and the One sitting on it. The earth and sky fled from His presence, but they found no place to hide. I saw the dead, both great and small, standing before God's throne. And the books were opened, including the Book of Life. And the dead were judged according to what they had done, as recorded in the books. The sea gave up its dead, and death and the grave gave up their dead. And all were judged according to their deeds. Then death and the grave were thrown into the lake of fire. This lake of fire is the second death. And anyone whose name was not found recorded in the Book of Life was thrown into the lake of fire."*

This is also referred to as the second death. In Revelation 20:4 there is reference to those beheaded for Christ during the Tribulation. They will be raised to life and rule with Christ during the Millennium. Verses 5 and 6 reads, *"This is the first resurrection. (The rest of the dead did not come back to life until the thousand years had ended.) Blessed and holy are those who share in the first resurrection. For them the second death holds no power, but they will be priests of God and of Christ and will reign with Him a thousand years."*

Let's break this down. The earth and sky fleeing from Jesus' presence indicates that this Great White Throne Judgement will take place someplace far away in space, away from the earth's atmosphere. There is speculation that perhaps this is the place of the black hole of space. There is also a theory that hell is located in this black hole. We don't know, of course; it's just speculation. Wherever this judgement takes place and wherever hell is located, I'm relieved we won't be witness to this horrible event. Unfortunately, some of our loved ones among others will be judged for their rejection of Jesus and will be cast away for eternity. I don't want to see this.

By the way, have you ever wondered how we can possibly have immeasurable joy when, perhaps, some those we have loved deeply may not be with us for eternity? I share three verses that answer this question:

1. Psalm 34:16 - *"But the Lord turns His face from those who do evil; He will erase their memory*

from the earth."

2. Job 18:17 - *"The memory of him perishes from the earth; he has no name in the land."*

3. Isaiah 65:17 - *"Look! I am creating new heavens and a new earth, and no one will even think about the old ones anymore."*

It is a tragic relief to know today that we will not be in sorrow for eternity because those who reject Christ will be erased from our memories. To those who do not yet know Jesus I implore you — please be remembered! Please accept the gift of forgiveness of sins from Jesus. Please call to Him. All those who love long for you to be remembered!

Let's now look at "the books" as mentioned above in Revelation 20:12b and 13b: "And the books were opened, including the Book of Life. And the dead were judged according to what they had done, as recorded in the books...And all were judged according to their deeds." There are actually two books.

One is the Book of Life. Every person from the moment of conception has their name written in the Book of Life. Only when rejection of Jesus and His saving grace takes place, is that name blotted out, erased for all time.

The second book is the Book of Deeds. Verse 12b tells us that the dead will be judged according to their deeds. I find God's great and perfect mercy evident even among those who reject Jesus. This is an indication that there are levels of punishment in hell. Don't think for a moment that any part of hell will be comfortable, but there are degrees of severity of punishment.

This brings us to another thought — are children in heaven? At what age are they held accountable for either acceptance or rejection of Christ? To begin with, remember what is written in II Peter 3:9: *"The Lord isn't really being slow concerning His promise, as some people think. No, He is being patient for your sake. He does not want anyone to be destroyed, but wants everyone to repent."* Further down the chapter in verse 15a Peter says, *"And remember, our Lord's patience gives people time to be saved."*

When we become Christians we long for Jesus to rapture us to be with Him always. His Father knows the right time. He waits until the last possible moment in order to give everyone that opportunity to receive Jesus Christ as their Savior. That's why we read in John 3:16 *"For God so loved the world that He gave His only begotten Son, that whosoever believes in Him should not perish but have everlasting life"* (King James version). God longs, with an immeasurable passion, that every living being receives His gift of salvation through His Son. Therefore, we can be absolutely certain that redeemed children are in heaven.

What is that age of accountability? There is no age given in God's Word. Some speculate it might be age twelve because that's the age of a Jewish boy's Bar Mitzvah, an important celebration which signifies the boy is now a man. However, that conjecture is not conclusive.

One thing we know for certain - God is fair, just, and full of mercy at all times. He knows each of us intimately. We do not all come to a point of maturity at the same time. Therefore, each child's age of accountability will be different. I've heard a pastor's testimony telling that at age four he understood his need for Jesus. I've heard other testimonies when the child was ten or twelve. I was 14 when I fully understood what Jesus had done for me and my need to repent and ask Him to save me. My own conclusion is that only God knows our hearts; only He is perfect in mercy and love. Therefore, we need not fear the question of the age a child is saved.

There is another question that is often asked about heaven: Can my loved ones see me? Are they watching over me? The short answer is, no, they cannot and are not, but I understand the sentiment here. This line of thought comes largely from Hebrews 12:1: *"Therefore, since we are surrounded by such a huge crowd of witnesses to the life of faith, let us strip off every weight that slows us down, especially the sin that so easily trips us up. And let us run with endurance the race God has set before us."*

The phrase, *"surrounded by such a huge crowd of witnesses,"* written in the King James Version as *"compassed about with so great a cloud of witnesses"* has made some imagine that their loved ones are looking down from a cloud or the heavens, watching us, encouraging us as we run our race. Again, I understand the sentiment, but the interpretation is incorrect.

Whenever we see the word "therefore" we know it is referring to something that has been said or done before. This reference is pointing back to all that has been said in Hebrews 11, which is often referred to as the faith chapter because it mentions so many of our Bible heroes. Their testimonies of faithfulness is an example to us. In other words, their own walks with Jesus makes them *witnesses* to us of the life of faith as stated in Hebrews 12:1. The verse is referring to them as witnesses as in giving their testimony (as in court) to the fact.

Keep in mind, also, that while it's a nice sentiment to think our loved ones are watching us and encouraging us, there is no one greater one to watch over and encourage us than the Holy Spirit. Your Heavenly Father is watching over you and me. Jesus brings our requests and needs to the Father. The Holy Spirit guides us into all truth.

We are now at a point in our study where we have come through the Millennium and The Great White Throne Judgment.

What happens next?

The most glorious part of all.

The New Heaven and the New Earth

John writes in Revelation 21:1: *"Then I saw a new heaven and a new earth, for the old heaven and the old earth had disappeared. And the sea was also gone."* You will notice that the word heaven is singular here, but you are probably aware that in other Bible verses heaven is plural. Let's look at two such verses.

1. Isaiah 65:17: *"Look! I am creating new heavens and a new earth, and no one will even think about the old ones anymore."*

2. II Peter 3:13: *"But we are looking forward to the new heavens and the new earth He has promised, a world filled with God's righteousness."*

The three heavens are as follows:

1. the earth's atmosphere

2. the planets

3. the location of the city of God

Revelation 21:1-4 refers to the City of God which we will look at later when we learn that the City of God, now in the third heaven, will come down into the earth's atmosphere. Therefore, it is one heaven, singular, referred to in this passage.

Continuing our look into the new heavens and new earth I bring your attention to Revelation 21:5: *"And the One sitting on the throne said, 'Look, I am making everything new!' And then He said to me, 'Write this down, for what I tell you is trustworthy and true.'"*

*W*hen we think of God making a new heaven and a new earth, we may well think of the present heaven or atmosphere, and the present earth, simply disappearing. We may imagine God speaking into existence a whole new heaven and earth. That's an understandable theory, but using our spiritual deep sea diving tools we learn this is not the case.

When we look into the original Greek we see that the word for "new" is KAHEE'MOS' which means new in quality or fresh in development or not exactly as before. I think of furniture refurbishing. Perhaps someone has an old chair. After years of use it has lost its beauty so it's taken to a professional who restores old furniture. The refurbisher may sand the wood, coat it with varnish, and apply new upholstery. The end result is a "new" chair, but of course, it's the old chair made better.

This is what we learn from the Greek word KAHEE-MOS'. The earth, which is now suffering due to man's misuse of its environment, will be refurbished. Pollution will be gone from earth as well from in the atmosphere. The singular use of heaven is referring to the immediate atmosphere of earth.

Let's look again at Revelation 21:1: "*... And the sea was also gone.*" For many years this rather saddened me. I love the ocean as many of you do. I believed the new heaven and new earth would indeed be wonderful, but I just couldn't understand why we couldn't have an ocean.

Also, if animals have life after death (I discuss animals in heaven in my book, <u>His Name Is Jack)</u> then wouldn't an ocean be needed for the whales, fish, and all sea life? For those reading this who feel the same disappointment I felt at "no more sea" read on. We're about to have disappointment turned into gladness.

We're about to delve into — The City Of God.

The City Of God

God's children have been aware of and looking forward to the City of God for a very long time. Hebrews 11:10 tells us, *"Abraham was confidently looking forward to a city with eternal foundations, a city designed and built by God."* I was both surprised and excited to discover that as far back as the time of Abraham, God's people were aware of a promised home that would literally be out of this world!

We don't actually know a lot about heaven and the City of God, but what we do know is amazing! For one thing, we have measurements of the city. But before we look at that, let's look at our own atmosphere. This will help us to imagine how grand the City of God is.

The NASA website gives lots of interesting information. One thing I discovered added to my excitement regarding the City of God. It concerns the layers of our atmosphere. They are as follows:

1. Troposphere - the area from the earth's surface extending 9 miles up

2. Stratosphere - extends 31 miles above the Troposphere where the UV rays are filtered through the ozone layer

3. Mesosphere - extends 53 miles above the Stratosphere, where meteorites hurling to earth are burned up

4. Thermosphere - extends 372 miles above the Mesosphere;

satellites orbit the earth in this sphere

5. Ionosphere - overlaps with the Mesosphere and Thermosphere; radio waves are found in this layer

6. Exosphere - the upper limit of our known atmosphere; begins at 6,200 miles above the earth and goes beyond into infinity

Now let's take a look at the measurements given for the City of God. In Revelation 21, John sees in his vision an angel measuring the City of God. John writes in Revelation 21:16, "When he measured it, he found it was a square, as wide as it was long. In fact, its length and width and height were each 1,400 *miles."* (According to the King James Version and Literal Emphasis Translation, the measurements were done in furlongs, cubits, and stadia. Thus the correlation is between 1400 and 1500 miles.)

Let's think further upon these measurements. Having looked at the different levels of the earth's atmosphere and its extension into space, we can better imagine the size of the City of God. Now consider this: In this city that is 1,500 miles high and wide, how many floors or levels are there? Is there a floor every mile or every half mile or quarter mile? We don't know, but doing the math we know that each floor will be an area of two million square miles!

When I first realized the size of the City of God and the area of each floor or level, my mouth fell open! It staggered me to imagine the greatness and splendor of this magnificent city that God is preparing for us. Do you better understand now, that indeed, there will be enough room for all of us and the animals?

One other thing I want to point out about the size and location of the City of God. There is a verse in Isaiah 66:1 that tells us, *"This is what the Lord says, 'Heaven is my throne and the earth is my footstool. Can you build me a temple as good as that? Can you build me such a resting place?'"* When I would read that verse, it conjured within me a sense of the awesomeness of God! How great is our God! However, as I came to understand more about heaven, and that the City of God hovers above the earth extending into space, I began to picture things more literally. God's throne will be in the City of God and the earth really will be His footstool! I had to share this thought — so exciting is what awaits us who know Him!

Right now the City of God is located in the third heaven. The Apostles Paul and John were given the great privilege of glimpsing this magnificent city. Remember, all Christians at the time of The Rapture will reside in the third heaven. Earth will be our place of work during the Millennium. At the end of the Millennium, after the Great White Throne Judgment has taken place, we read in Revelation 21:10: *"So he took me in the Spirit to a great, high mountain. and he showed me the holy city, Jerusalem, descending out of heaven from God."* In verse two of this same chapter, we read *"And I saw the holy city, the new Jerusalem, coming down from God out of heaven like a bride beautifully dressed for her husband."*

During the Millennium, Jesus will take His rightful place in Jerusalem, sitting on the throne of David. Jerusalem will be the earth's capital. After the Millennium, The City of God comes down to the earth's atmosphere and will be the New Jerusalem. This new city is more beautiful than anything seen thus far. We are given particulars in Revelation 21:11-21 as follows:

- The entire city sparked like jasper and is as clear as glass - v.11

- There are twelve gates in the city, three on each side with the names of the twelve tribes of

Israel written on them - vs.12-13

- The walls have twelve foundation stones, each with the names of the twelve apostles - v.14

- The walls are 216 feet thick - v. 17

- The walls are made of jasper and the city is of pure gold, as clear as glass - v.18

- The twelve stones are: jasper, sapphire, agate, emerald, onyx, carnelian, chrysolite, beryl, topaz, chrysoprase, jacinth, amethyst - vs.19-20

- The twelves gates are each made of one single pearl! The main street is gold as clear as glass -

v.21

The rest of Revelation 21 tells us that there will be no sun or moon because God's glory illuminates the city and the Lamb is its light. The gates are never closed because it's never night. People from every nation will live there, all whose names are written in the Book of Life. It is for that reason that the City of God will not yet come down to the earth's atmosphere during the Millennium. Only God's children will ever see it.

In Revelation 22:1-2 we read something that can be rather confusing. *"Then the angel showed me a river with the water of life, clear as crystal, flowing from the throne of God and of the Lamb. It flowed down to the center of the main street. On each side of the river grew a tree of life, bearing twelve crops of fruit, with a fresh crop each month. The leaves were used for medicine to heal the nations."* There was a time I would read these verses and be so confused. Questions swirled in my brain, for example, if there's no death or sickness in heaven, then why are there leaves that provide healing for the nations? Have you ever wondered the same thing?

First, let's go back to Genesis where the tree of life is first mentioned. In chapter three we see that Adam and Eve have chosen to sin against God. As a result, they have been banned from the Garden of Eden. In Genesis 3:24 we read, *"After sending them out, the Lord God stationed mighty cherubim to the east of the Garden of Eden. And He placed a flaming sword that flashed back and forth to guard the way to the tree of life."* This was not a cruel or severe punishment; this was a great mercy, a severe love. If Adam and Eve were to eat from the tree of life in their now fallen state, they would be in that state for eternity. In His great and perfect love, God forbid that to happen. From that moment, mankind could only come to God and have the privilege of eating from the tree of life in the City of God after receiving the gift of salvation through His son Jesus Christ. Remember, those in the Old Testament were saved by faith in the coming Messiah, Jesus. Those in the New Testament and forever thereafter, are saved by faith in the already come, died, and resurrected Messiah, Jesus.

Coming back to Revelation 22 we discover that the tree of life is an orchard! More than one tree growing on each side of the river with the water of life, bearing a different fruit each month. So what is the meaning of the fruit and the leaves providing healing for the nations? We must use our tools to discover the meaning.

The word "heal" used here in verse three is the original Greek word THERAPEIA. It is from this word that we get our English word - therapy. It means to enhance a sense of well being. I explain it this way: as I write this I am in good health. I feel well all over. I'm thankful to say I have no aches and pains. As far as I am aware, everything on the inside is also doing well. However, as well as I feel, if someone were to come up behind me, place their hands on my shoulders and begin to massage my shoulders and neck, I would be uttering an aaaahhhhhhhh sound. It would feel so good! In other words, my already healthy, feeling good self, would now be enhanced. That is what the Greek word THERAPEIA denotes. Isn't that wonderful? I can hardly wait to experience this!

Let's also talk about the *"river with the water of life, clear as crystal, flowing from the throne of God and of the Lamb."* Remember, every floor of the City of God is an area of two million square miles. Where in the city is the throne of God? We don't know. Is it at the top with the river beginning wide and flowing down through all the floors? Does it cascade onto the earth? We don't know, but can you imagine the splendor? Can you now imagine how the whales and other sea life won't need salt water to survive? Can you now envision being more than satisfied with this river rather than *"no more sea"* mentioned in Revelation 21:1? As I shared earlier, as much as I love the ocean, I am certain I will not miss it when I see in its place the river with water of life, clear as crystal.

Conclusion

Dear readers, we have now come to the end of our study of Satan's tactics and how to be aware of his lies, and the importance of preparing for The Rapture so we are not caught embarrassed at His coming. We have glimpsed into what we know of the coming Tribulation, Millennium, and the glorious City of God. I have prayed for each of you to be empowered by the Holy Spirit through all your days.

"Look, I am coming soon, bringing my reward with me to repay all people according to their deeds. I am the Alpha and the Omega, the First and the Last, the Beginning and the End. Blessed are those who wash their robes. They will be permitted to enter through the gates of the city and eat the fruit

from the tree of life" **(Revelation 22:12-14).**

At A Glance - End Times Chronological Events

1. **The Rapture** - The sudden disappearance of all Christians, the dead in Christ first and those who are alive, meet Jesus in the air.

2. **Judgement Seat of Christ** - The Marriage Banquet of Jesus the husband, with His bride the church. Rewards will be given for all we have done on earth. We then have something to give back in worship.

425

3. **Tribulation -** Seven years of terror such as the world has never seen thus far. Weather catastrophes, famines, plagues. The greatest persecution of Christians but also the greatest revival. The Antichrist comes to power. The beast requires worship of the Antichrist by wearing the mark 666. Armageddon takes place in Israel as the Antichrist sits on the throne of David.

4. **Millennium** - Christ sets foot on the Mount of Olives, removes the Antichrist, the beast, and Satan from the scene. Jesus takes His rightful place on the throne of David and rules for one thousand years of peace such as the world has never seen. Resurrected Christians, living among regular

humans, will rule in all places of authority and leadership. At the very end, Satan is loosed for a short time when he will join Russia for one last attempt to overthrow Jesus. Satan is immediately quashed, thus ending sin on earth for eternity.

5. **Great White Throne Judgment** - Every person who has rejected Jesus will be judged, found guilty, and cast into Hell for eternity. They will be erased from the memory of all Christians.

6. **The City of God** - This magnificent city, the home of every Christian, will drop to the earth's atmosphere, making the earth its footstool. The river of God will flow from the Throne of

God with fruit from the tree of life changing each month. The fruit will be an enhancement to our already perfect bodies. There are many floors, each an area of approximately two million square miles. The city is made of gold and pearls and every precious stone. Jesus is the light so no sun or moon is needed. There is never again any sorrow or pain or tears. Eternal joy with Jesus will be the inheritance of every Christian.

Bibliography of References

Commentaries

1. Barnes Bible Notes

2. Chuck Blair Bible Notes (non published)

3. Matthew Henry Commentary

4. Pulpit Commentary

5. Vernon McGee Bible Notes

Bible Study Tools

1. New Living Translation Bible

2. Greek-English Interlinear New Testament

3. King James Translation Bible

4. Literal Emphasis Translation Bible

5. Manners and Customs of Bible Times, Ralph R Gower

6. New Testament Greek Lexicon

7. Old Testament Hebrew Lexicon

8. Strong's Concordance

9. Unger's Bible Handbook

10. Vine's Expository Dictionary of Old and New Testament Words

11. Wuest's Word Studies in the Greek New Testament

Spiritual Warfare Books

1. Strategy of Satan, Warren W. Wiersbe

2. Surprised by the Power of the Spirit, Jack Deere

3. The Battle Is The Lord's, Tony Evans

4. Whatever Happened To The Power of God, Michael L. Brown

5. When Pigs Move In, Don Dickerman

6. Word and Spirit, Paul Cain & R.T. Kendall

End Times Books

1. Agents of Babylon, David Jeremiah

2. Be Victorious, Warren W. Wiersbe

3. Book of Signs, David Jeremiah

4. Daniel-End Time Mysteries Unsealed, Jack Van Impe

5. Is This The End?, David Jeremiah

6. When Christ Appears, David Jeremiah

7. Revealing The Mysteries of Heaven, David Jeremiah

8. Revelation Revealed, Jack Van Impe

Internet Sources

1. www.nasa.gov

2. www.biblehub.org

Other Books By Vickie J Blair

1. With Wings Life An Eagle

2. Back On The Potter's Wheel

3. Developing Your Spiritual Eyesight

4. A Year Not Wanted

5. The Great Cascade

6. Life On Ellinnet Road

7. Avoiding Shipwreck

8. Mommy, Can You Feel Me?

9. Lambie Of Chipangali

10. Grandpa Rooster and His Silver Treasure Chest

11. Molly Moo and Her Hair Raising, Frightful, Very Scary Day

12.His Name Is Jack

By Chuck Blair

Reflections of The Old Tabernacle In the
New Testament

Printed in Great Britain
by Amazon